Steck-Vaughn

REV it up!

Robust Encounters with Vocabulary

Isabel L. Beck, Ph.D., and
Margaret G. McKeown, Ph.D.

Steck Vaughn™

HOUGHTON MIFFLIN HARCOURT
Supplemental Publishers

www.SteckVaughn.com
800-531-5015

Acknowledgments

Literature

Grateful acknowledgment is given to the following publishers and copyright owners for permissions granted to reprint selections from their publications. All possible care has been taken to trace ownership and secure permission for each selection included. In the case of any errors or omissions, the Publisher will be pleased to make suitable acknowledgments in future editions.

p. 9, From INTO THIN AIR by Jon Krakauer, copyright © 1997 by Jon Krakauer. Used by permission of Villard Books, a division of Random House, Inc.

p. 22, from "The Rain Came" from *Land Without Thunder* by Grace Ogot. Reproduced with permission from East African Educational Publishers Ltd.

p. 35, "My Dad, King of Cool" by Carlos Sanchez, copyright © 2001 by Austin American-Statesman. Reprinted with permission.

p. 48, "A Picture of My Mother's Family" from EXPOUNDING THE DOUBTFUL POINTS by Wing Tek Lum. Reprinted by permission of the author.

p. 73, From THE MAN IN THE WATER by Roger Rosenblatt, copyright © 1994 by Roger Rosenblatt. Used by permission of Random House, Inc.

p. 85, "The Anatomy Lesson" © 1981 by Scott Russell Sanders; reprinted by permission of the author.

p. 96, Quote by Mohandas K. Gandhi. Reprinted by permission of the Navajivan Trust.

p. 99, "Bigfoot in Texas? Believers, Skeptics Sound Off at Institute" by Richard A. Lovett, reprinted by permission of The National Geographic Society.

p. 111, Pages 34-36 (with two words changed) from "Transformation" from TALKING TO HIGH MONKS IN THE SNOW by LYDIA MINATOYA Copyright © 1992 by Lydia Minatoya. Reprinted by permission of HarperCollins Publishers.

p. 123, From LONG WALK TO FREEDOM by NELSON MANDELA. Copyright © 1994, 1995 by Nelson Rolihlahla Mandela. By permission of Little, Brown and Co., Inc.

p. 148, from My Left Foot by Christy Brown, published by Secker & Warburg. Reprinted by permission of The Random House Group Ltd.

p. 160, "Reflections on History in Missouri" from *Lone Woman and Others,* by Constance Urdang, © 1980. Reprinted by permission of the University of Pittsburgh Press.

p. 161, "My Arkansas", copyright © 1978 by Maya Angelou, from AND STILL I RISE by Maya Angelou. Used by permission of Random House, Inc.

p. 184, "My Two Dads" by Marie G. Lee. Reprinted by permission of the author.

Cover photo ©Brad Wrobleski/Masterfile www.masterfile.com.

Acknowledgments for photography and illustrations can be found on page 216.

ISBN-13: 978-1-4190-4041-2
ISBN-10:   1-4190-4041-3

Printed in China 4 5 6 7 8 9 10 0940 13 12 11
4500288935

Contents

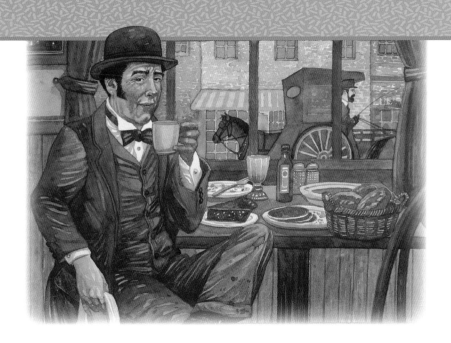

from

INTO THIN AIR

By Jon Krakauer

Blinded by their determination to reach the top of Mt. Everest, members of the doomed 1996 expedition failed to notice the killer storm developing until it was too late.

Straddling the top of the world, one foot in China and the other in Nepal, I cleared the ice from my oxygen mask, hunched a shoulder against the wind, and stared absently down at the vastness of Tibet. I understood on some dim, detached level that the sweep of earth beneath my feet was a spectacular sight. I'd been fantasizing about this moment, and the release of emotion that would accompany it, for many months. But now that I was finally here, actually standing on the summit of Mount Everest, I just couldn't summon the energy to care.

It was early in the afternoon of May 10, 1996. I hadn't slept in fifty-seven hours. The only food I'd been able to force down over the preceding three days was a bowl of ramen soup and a handful of peanut M&Ms. Weeks of violent coughing had left me with two separated ribs that made ordinary breathing an excruciating trial. At 29,028 feet up in the troposphere,[1] so little oxygen was reaching my brain that my mental capacity was that of a slow child. Under the circumstances, I was incapable of feeling much of anything except cold and tired.

I'd arrived on the summit a few minutes after Anatoli Boukreev, a Russian climbing guide working for an American commercial expedition, and just ahead of Andy Harris, a guide on the New Zealand-based team to which I belonged. Although I was only slightly acquainted with Boukreev, I'd come to know and like Harris well during the preceding six weeks. I snapped four quick photos of Harris and Boukreev striking summit poses, then turned and headed down. My watch read 1:17 P.M. All told, I'd spent less than five minutes on the roof of the world.[2]

A moment later, I paused to take another photo, this one looking down on the Southeast Ridge, the route we had ascended. Training my lens[3] on a pair of climbers approaching the summit, I noticed something that until that moment had escaped my attention. To the south, where the sky had been perfectly clear just an hour earlier, a blanket of clouds now hid Pumori, Ama Dablam, and the other lesser peaks surrounding Everest.

FOOTNOTES
1 *troposphere:* lowest layer of the atmosphere
2 *roof of the world:* highest point on Earth
3 *training my lens:* focusing my camera

Later—after six bodies had been located, after a search for two others had been abandoned, after surgeons had amputated the gangrenous[4] right hand of my teammate Beck Weathers—people would ask why, if the weather had begun to deteriorate, had climbers on the upper mountain not heeded the signs? Why did veteran Himalayan guides keep moving upward, ushering a gaggle[5] of relatively inexperienced amateurs—each of whom had paid as much as $65,000 to be taken safely up Everest—into an apparent death trap?

Nobody can speak for the leaders of the two guided groups involved, because both men are dead. But I can attest that nothing I saw early on the afternoon of May 10 suggested that a murderous storm was bearing down. To my oxygen-depleted mind, the clouds drifting up the grand valley of ice known as the Western Cwm looked innocuous, wispy, insubstantial. Gleaming in the brilliant midday sun, they appeared no different from the harmless puffs of convection condensation that rose from the valley almost every afternoon.

As I began my descent I was extremely anxious, but my concern had little to do with the weather: a check of the gauge on my oxygen tank had revealed that it was almost empty. I needed to get down, fast.

The uppermost shank[6] of Everest's Southeast Ridge is a slender, heavily corniced fin[7] of rock and wind-scoured snow that snakes for a quarter mile between the summit and a subordinate pinnacle known as the South Summit. Negotiating the serrated ridge presents no great technical hurdles, but the route is dreadfully exposed. After leaving the summit, fifteen minutes of cautious shuffling over a 7,000-foot abyss brought me to the notorious Hillary Step, a pronounced notch in the ridge that demands some technical maneuvering. As I clipped into a fixed rope and prepared to rappel[8] over the lip, I was greeted with an alarming sight.

Thirty feet below, more than a dozen people were queued up[9] at the base of the Step. Three climbers were already in the process of hauling themselves up the rope that I was preparing to descend. Exercising my only option, I unclipped from the communal safety line and stepped aside.

FOOTNOTES

[4] *gangrenous:* decaying
[5] *ushering a gaggle:* guiding a noisy group
[6] *shank:* long, narrow part
[7] *corniced fin:* iced ridge
[8] *rappel:* lower oneself using a rope
[9] *queued up:* lined up

The traffic jam was comprised of climbers from three expeditions: the team I belonged to, a group of paying clients under the leadership of the celebrated New Zealand guide Rob Hall; another guided party headed by the American Scott Fischer; and a noncommercial Taiwanese team. Moving at the snail's pace that is the norm above 26,000 feet, the throng labored up the Hillary Step one by one, while I nervously bided my time.[10]

Harris, who'd left the summit shortly after I did, soon pulled up behind me. Wanting to conserve whatever oxygen remained in my tank, I asked him to reach inside my backpack and turn off the valve on my regulator, which he did. For the next ten minutes I felt surprisingly good. My head cleared. I actually seemed less tired than I had with the gas turned on. Then, abruptly, I sensed that I was suffocating. My vision dimmed and my head began to spin. I was on the brink of losing consciousness.

Instead of turning my oxygen off, Harris, in his hypoxically impaired[11] state, had mistakenly cranked the valve open to full flow, draining the tank. I'd just squandered the last of my gas going nowhere. There was another tank waiting for me at the South Summit, 250 feet below, but to get there I would have to descend the most exposed terrain on the entire route without the benefit of supplemental oxygen.

And first I had to wait for the mob to disperse. I removed my now useless mask, planted my ice ax into the mountain's frozen hide, and hunkered on the ridge. As I exchanged banal congratulations with the climbers filing past, inwardly I was frantic: "Hurry it up, hurry it up!" I silently pleaded. . . .

Most of the passing crowd belonged to Fischer's group, but near the back of the parade two of my teammates eventually appeared, Rob Hall and Yasuko Namba. Demure and reserved, the forty-seven-year-old Namba was forty minutes away from becoming the oldest woman to climb Everest and the second Japanese woman to reach the highest point on each continent, the so-called Seven Summits. Although she weighed just ninety-one pounds, her sparrowlike proportions disguised a formidable resolve; to an astounding degree, Yasuko had been propelled up the mountain by the unwavering intensity of her desire. . . .

FOOTNOTES
[10] *bided my time:* waited patiently
[11] *hypoxically impaired:* not thinking clearly because of a lack of oxygen

At the very end of the line was Scott Fischer, whom I knew casually from Seattle, where we both lived. Fischer's strength and drive were legendary—in 1994 he'd climbed Everest without using bottled oxygen—so I was surprised at how slowly he was moving and how hammered he looked when he pulled his mask aside to say hello. "Bruuuuuuuce!" he wheezed with forced cheer, employing his trademark frat-boyish greeting. When I asked how he was doing, Fischer insisted that he was feeling fine: "Just dragging . . . a little today for some reason. No big deal." With the Hillary Step finally clear, I clipped into the strand of orange rope, swung quickly around Fischer as he slumped over his ice ax, and rappelled over the edge.

It was after three o'clock when I made it down to the South Summit. By now tendrils of mist were streaming over the 27,923-foot top of Lhotse and lapping at Everest's summit pyramid. No longer did the weather look so benign. I grabbed a fresh oxygen cylinder, jammed it onto my regulator, and hurried down into the gathering cloud. Moments after I dropped below the South Summit, it began to snow lightly and visibility [was lost].

Four hundred vertical feet above, where the summit was still washed in bright sunlight under an immaculate cobalt sky, my compadres[12] dallied[13] to memorialize their arrival at the apex[14] of the planet, unfurling flags and snapping photos, using up precious ticks of the clock. None of them imagined that a horrible ordeal was drawing nigh.[15] Nobody suspected that by the end of that long day, every minute would matter.

FOOTNOTES
....
[12] *compadres:* friends
[13] *dallied:* wasted time
[14] *apex:* highest point
[15] *drawing nigh:* about to happen

Explain Yourself

Answer each question on a separate piece of paper. Be sure to explain your answers.

1. What kind of animals would be able to **ascend** a tree? Why?

2. Would you want your voice to **deteriorate** during a school concert? Why or why not?

3. How would you feel if the supply of tickets to your favorite concert were **depleted**? Explain.

4. Do you think video games are **innocuous**? Why or why not?

5. What would the plot of a **banal** novel be like? Explain.

6. Would you act **demurely** around someone you had a crush on? Why or why not?

7. When would you want to make yourself look **formidable**? Why?

8. For what event would you want to look **immaculate**? Explain.

9. What kind of after-school job would be **arduous**? Explain.

10. What could make a person **err** while driving? Explain.

ascend Something that ascends moves upward.

deteriorate If something deteriorates, its condition gets worse and worse.

deplete When supplies are depleted, they are completely used up.

innocuous Something that is innocuous won't hurt you because it is harmless.

banal Someone or something that is banal is so common that it is boring.

demure A demure person is quiet and shy.

formidable If someone or something is formidable, you feel threatened by its size or strength.

immaculate Something that is immaculate is spotlessly clean.

arduous An arduous task takes a lot of effort.

err If you err, you make a mistake.

Take It Further

Complete these sentences on a separate piece of paper.

1. At the mall, Sasha **ascended** . . .

2. Our teamwork **deteriorated** because . . .

3. Madelyn's allowance was **depleted** because . . .

4. Although the cafeteria food looked **innocuous**, it . . .

5. That new song is really **banal** because . . .

6. We all thought Trinh was **demure** until she . . .

7. Mark's violin performance was **formidable** because . . .

8. Felix's teeth were **immaculate** after . . .

9. Our science project was **arduous** because . . .

10. Because Zulema didn't want to **err** while giving her speech, she . . .

Explore It

You know the word *err* means "to make a mistake," but did you notice that *err* sounds very similar to the word *air*? What if you replaced one word with the other?

Some athletes use the phrase *big air* to describe a huge skiing or snowboarding jump. If you changed this phrase to *big err,* it might mean "a huge snowboarding mistake!" Think of a word, phrase, or sentence that contains the word *air.* Now replace the word *air* with the word *err.* Write a definition of your new phrase and illustrate the definition. Challenge a partner to figure out what your new phrase means.

Use the following suggestions or think of some of your own: *err*plane, *err*port, *err* bag.

Sending Mozart
to the STARS

Y ou probably listen to your favorite CDs or MP3s with your friends, but have you ever shared music with an alien?

Scientists from NASA filled an immaculate golden disc with music and pictures designed to show beings in outer space what Earth is like. The disc, called the Golden Record, ascended into space in 1977 with the help of two spacecrafts, Voyager 1 and 2. Right now, it's traveling beyond our solar system in search of alien life.

The record contains 115 pictures of Earth and a lot of natural sounds, like thunder, waves, and bird calls. It also holds recordings of 55 different languages and about 90 minutes of music.

Don't expect to get a response from the aliens asking for more music after they've depleted the supply—it's not expected to reach other planets for 40,000 years. If alien beings exist at all and do find it, though, let's hope they like what they hear.

FACT:

The inventor of a torpedo-shaped box filled with items for future humans to discover originally called his box a "time bomb." When people decided that this name was inappropriate, he made up a new one. The first "time capsule" was born.

FACT:

Imagine writing an e-mail to yourself today . . . and getting it when you're 35! In 2005, a magazine collected letters that its readers wrote to themselves. The magazine will e-mail the letters back to the readers at some point during the next 20 years.

Make Your Own Time Capsule

1. Find a container, preferably one made from stainless steel or aluminum.

2. Find some things to put in your time capsule. You can include special items, like a trophy, or more banal stuff like postcards. Write a letter to your future self or download your favorite photos to a CD.

3. Put each item in its own sealed plastic bag or acid-free container to keep it from deteriorating.

4. Label your time capsule. Put it in a plastic bag and store it in a safe place indoors or bury it on your own property.

5. Decide when you want to open the capsule. When it's time to recover it, you'll enjoy getting a blast from the past!

Graduation photos

Postcard from Colorado

COLORADO

Tori, Jenna, Joci, and Mike—Colorado skiing trip

Rev Up Your Writing

Time capsules can send information about our everyday lives far into the future. If you had to put three things into a time capsule, what would you choose? What would you want people in the future to find out about life as you know it? Use as many of the vocabulary words as possible but make sense.

Word Organizer

Copy this graphic organizer onto a separate piece of paper.

List events that you would find banal in the top half of the Word Wheel. List events that are not banal in the bottom half.

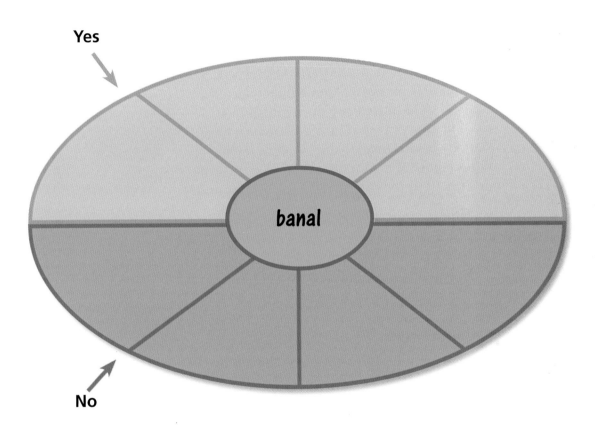

Yes

banal

No

X Marks the Spot

Here are two tales of hidden treasure. Are you up to the arduous task of finding the treasure for yourself?

Treasure #1: Captain Kidd's Loot

It's said that pirate William Kidd collected a huge amount of treasure during his life at sea. He's the only real pirate known to have actually buried his treasure. People say he buried most of his loot on an island "east of Boston," but the treasure's never been found.

Find It Yourself! Try searching Clark's Island in Massachusetts or Oak Island in Nova Scotia, Canada. Don't err during your search, though. The islands might look innocuous, but Oak Island has a mysterious "treasure pit" guarded with traps.

Treasure #2: The Beale Gold

In the 1800s, the story goes, Thomas Beale discovered gold and silver near Santa Fe, New Mexico. He buried the treasure and wrote three coded messages describing its location. Before he could explain how to decode the messages, he vanished forever.

Find It Yourself! Look on the Internet or in your library for copies of Beale's coded messages. One message has already been figured out, but the others remain a mystery. If you crack the final two codes, you'll know where the treasure is. Good luck!

Is a Pirate's Life for You?

Take this quiz to find out!

1 What do you do with money?
   a) I give it all to charity.
   b) I keep it in my wallet or the bank.
   c) I put it in a chest, mark it with a
      giant X, and bury it.

2 What kind of pet do you have?
   a) I don't have a pet.
   b) I have a cat, a dog, or a fish.
   c) I have a parrot that sits on my shoulder
      and tells me mates what to do.

3 How do you spend your free time?
   a) I hang out at the mall.
   b) I go to the beach.
   c) I sail the sea in search of me treasure.

4 What would you do if you found a buried
treasure?
   a) How should I know?
   b) Um . . . share it with my friends?
   c) Work *arrrrduously* to hide it so no one
      shall ever find it!

5 Translate this sentence: *Avast, me
hearties, thar be scurvy corsairs
makin' off with the booty!*
   a) A big-hearted and curvy
      horse is taking off his boots!
   b) Translate it to what?
   c) Hey, guys, some other pirates
      are taking the treasure!

Quiz Results:

mostly As: You're much too demure to be a pirate.
Why not consider another profession?

mostly Bs: You'd make a fine pirate. With practice,
you'll be a formidable buccaneer.

mostly Cs: Shiver me timbers! Ye already
are a true pirate!

Rev Up Your Writing

To a pirate, a treasure might be piles of
gold and jewels, but other people might
treasure different things. Write about
what you consider a treasure to be.
Does it have to be something expensive
or something you can touch? Use as
many vocabulary words as possible but
make sense.

Can You Relate?

Copy this graphic organizer onto a separate piece of paper. Match the following words with their related vocabulary word. If a word relates to more than one vocabulary word, explain why.

attribute An attribute is a quality or trait that someone has.
laconic If you are laconic, you don't say very much.
legion A legion of people or things is a large number of them.
omnipotent If you are omnipotent, you have complete power.
serenity If you experience serenity, you feel peaceful and calm.

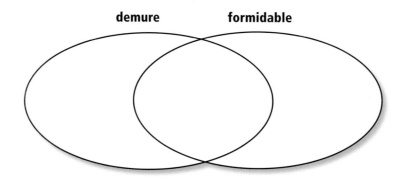

In Your Own Words

Respond to one of the following prompts on a separate piece of paper. As you respond, use as many of the vocabulary words as possible. Be creative but make sense!

▶ Write about a time when you or someone you know had to complete a challenging physical activity. What motivated you to finish the activity? How did it make you feel?

▶ Write a short story about a character who travels to the future. Who (or what) does the character meet? Is the future very different from the present or is it surprisingly similar?

▶ Write about a topic of your choice.

VOCABULARY

ascend
deteriorate
deplete
innocuous
banal
demure
formidable
immaculate
arduous
err

from

The Rain Came

By Grace Ogot
Illustrated by Diana Kizlauskas

The chief of an African village learns he must sacrifice his only daughter to a monster to bring much-needed rain to his village. Will the daughter be willing to die to save her friends and family?

The chief was still far from the gate when his daughter Oganda saw him. She ran to meet him. Breathlessly she asked her father, "What is the news, great Chief? Everyone in the village is anxiously waiting to hear when it will rain." Labong'o held out his hands for his daughter but he did not say a word. . . .

Labong'o went to his own hut, a sign that he was not to be disturbed. Having replaced the shutter, he sat in the dimly-lit hut to contemplate.[1]

It was no longer a question of being the chief of hunger-stricken people that weighed Labong'o's heart.[2] It was the life of his only daughter that was at stake. At the time when Oganda came to meet him, he saw the glittering chain shining around her waist. The prophecy was complete. "It is Oganda, Oganda, my only daughter, who must die so young." Labong'o burst into tears before finishing the sentence. . . .

The words of Ndithi, the medicine man,[3] still echoed in his ears.

". . . Out of all the women in this land, we have chosen this one. Let her offer herself a sacrifice to the lake monster! And on that day, the rain will come down in torrents. . . . "

. . . Labong'o removed his crown and the large eagle-head that hung loosely on his shoulders. He left the hut, and instead of asking Nyabog'o the messenger to beat the drum, he went straight and beat it himself. In no time the whole household had assembled under the siala tree[4] where he usually addressed them. He told Oganda to wait a while in her grandmother's hut.

When Labong'o stood to address his household, his voice was hoarse and the tears choked him. He started to speak, but words refused to leave his lips. . . . At last he told them. "One whom we love and treasure must be taken away from us. Oganda is to die." Labong'o's voice was so faint, that he could not hear it himself. But he continued, "The ancestors have chosen her to be offered as a sacrifice to the lake monster in order that we may have rain."

They were completely stunned. As a confused murmur broke out, Oganda's mother fainted and was carried off to her own hut. But the other people rejoiced. They danced around singing and chanting, "Oganda is the lucky one to die for the people. If it is to save the people, let Oganda go."

FOOTNOTES
....
1 *contemplate:* think long and hard
2 *weighed Labong'o's heart:* gave him great sadness
3 *medicine man:* in some cultures, a person who practices healing
4 *siala tree:* a tree that grows in East Africa

In her grandmother's hut Oganda wondered what the whole family were discussing about her that she could not hear. . . . "It must be marriage," she concluded. It was an accepted custom for the family to discuss their daughter's future marriage behind her back. A faint smile played on Oganda's lips. . . .

Oganda fingered the glittering chain on her waist as she thought of Osinda. A long time ago when she was quite young Osinda had given her that chain, and instead of wearing it around her neck several times, she wore it round her waist where it could stay permanently. She heard her heart pounding so loudly as she thought of him. She whispered, "Let it be you they are discussing, Osinda, the lovely one. Come now and take me away . . ."

The lean figure in the doorway startled Oganda who was rapt in thought about the man she loved. "You have frightened me, Grandma," said Oganda laughing. "Tell me, is it my marriage you were discussing? . . ."

In the open space outside the excited relatives were dancing and singing. They were coming to the hut now, each carrying a gift to put at Oganda's feet. As their singing got nearer Oganda was able to hear what they were saying: "If it is to save the people, if it is to give us rain, let Oganda go. Let Oganda die for her people, and for her ancestors." . . . Oganda . . . suddenly felt panicky like a mouse cornered by a hungry cat. Forgetting that there was only one door in the hut Oganda fought desperately to find another exit. She must fight for her life. But there was none. . . .

In the morning a big feast was prepared for Oganda. . . . Delicious though the food looked, Oganda touched none of it. . . .

The time for her departure was drawing near. . . . From the time Oganda received the sad news she had expected Osinda to appear any moment. But he was not there. A relative told her that Osinda was away on a private visit. Oganda realised that she would never see her beloved again.

In the afternoon the whole village stood at the gate to say good-bye and to see her for the last time. . . . The crowd looked at Oganda sympathetically, mumbling words she could not hear. But none of them pleaded for life. . . .

Oganda held her breath as she crossed the barrier to enter the sacred land. She looked appealingly at the crowd, but there was no response. Their minds were too preoccupied with their own survival. . . .

A strange feeling possessed Oganda as she picked her way in the sacred land. There were strange noises that often startled her, and her first reaction was to take to her heels.[5] But she remembered that she had to fulfill the wish of her people. She was exhausted, but the path was still winding. Then suddenly the path ended on sandy land. The water had retreated miles away from the shore leaving a wide stretch of sand. Beyond this was the vast expanse of water.

Oganda felt afraid. She wanted to picture the size and shape of the monster, but fear would not let her. . . . For a long time Oganda walked ankle-deep in the sand. . . . As she moved on, she had a strange feeling that something was following her. Was it the monster? Her hair stood erect, and a cold paralyzing feeling ran along her spine. She looked behind, sideways and in front, but there was nothing, except a cloud of dust. . . .

Oganda started to run. . . . As she ran she heard a noise coming from behind. She looked back sharply, and something resembling a moving bush was frantically running after her. It was about to catch up with her.

Oganda ran with all her strength. . . . She did not look back, but the creature was upon her. She made an effort to cry out, as in a nightmare, but she could not hear her own voice. . . . As Oganda came face to face with the unidentified creature, a strong hand grabbed her. But she fell flat on the sand and fainted.

When the lake breeze brought her back to consciousness, a man was bending over her. . . .

"Osinda, Osinda! Please let me die. . . . Let me die, let them have rain." Osinda fondled the glittering chain around Oganda's waist and wiped the tears from her face.

"We must escape quickly to the unknown land," Osinda said urgently. "We must run away from the wrath of the ancestors and the retaliation of the monster."

. . . Oganda broke loose, afraid to escape, but Osinda grabbed her hands again.

FOOTNOTES
[5] *take to her heels:* run away

"Listen to me, Oganda! Listen! Here are two coats!" He then covered the whole of Oganda's body, except her eyes, with a leafy attire made from the twigs of *Bwombwe*.[6] "These will protect us from the eyes of the ancestors and the wrath of the monster. Now let us run out of here." He held Oganda's hand and they ran from the sacred land. . . .

There was a bright lightening. They looked up, frightened. Above them black furious clouds started to gather. . . . Then the thunder roared, and the rain came down in torrents.

FOOTNOTES
....
[6] *Bwombwe:* an African tree with thick limbs and leaves

Explain Yourself

VOCABULARY

Answer each question on a separate piece of paper. Be sure to explain your answers.

1. What would you do if your friend was **stricken** with something? Explain.

2. How would you survive if you were caught in a **torrent**? Explain.

3. What kind of movie would make you **rapt**? Why?

4. How might you be **preoccupied** by a new pet? Why?

5. What is the most valuable item that you **possess**? Explain.

6. Where in your town could you see an **expanse**? Explain.

7. How would you **retaliate** if a friend hit you with a confetti egg? Explain.

8. How could you **ameliorate** a friend's hurt feelings? Explain.

9. Why might you **capitulate** to your friend if he asked you for money?

10. In what situation would you act **furtively**? Explain.

stricken   If you are stricken with something, you are suffering from it.

torrent   A torrent is a large amount of fast and furiously flowing water.

rapt   If you are rapt, something amazes you and captures your attention.

preoccupied   When you're preoccupied with something, you are thinking about it so much that you don't notice other things.

possess   If you possess something, you own it and control it.

expanse   An expanse is a wide, open area.

retaliate   When you retaliate, you get revenge for something that someone has done to you.

ameliorate   Someone who ameliorates a situation makes it better or easier.

capitulate   When you capitulate, you give up and surrender.

furtive   Furtive people are secretive and sneaky because they are trying to hide what they are doing.

Take It Further

Complete these sentences on a separate piece of paper.

1. Jana could tell her mom was **stricken** when she . . .

2. While Jorge was in the **torrent,** he felt . . .

3. My dog was held **rapt** by . . .

4. Lucy could tell her aunt was **preoccupied** because . . .

5. Someday I would like to **possess** . . .

6. The **expanse** of the field was perfect for . . .

7. Jason made Carlos want to **retaliate** because . . .

8. Andrea tried to **ameliorate** the argument by . . .

9. During the soccer game, Alex's team finally **capitulated** when . . .

10. The **furtive** students were trying to . . .

Explore It

You know the word *rapt* by now, but did you notice that *rapt* sounds a lot like the word *wrapped* (as in "I wrapped a present")? It also sounds like *rapped,* which can mean "knocked quickly" or "performed rap music." The words *rapt, wrapped,* and *rapped* are homonyms, which means they sound the same but have different meanings.

With a partner, write a short rap. The rap can be about anything you'd like, but it has to include each of the words *rapped, wrapped,* and *rapt* at least once. When you're done writing, perform your rap for the class. For an extra twist, try to illustrate the homonyms as you say them. For example, when you reach the word *rapped* in your rap, keep acting like a rapper, but start knocking quickly on a wall or desk. If you say the word *wrapped,* start acting like you're wrapping a present or wrap yourself in a jacket. And when you say *rapt,* act amazed and captivated.

The CROCODILE Hunter

You may recognize the khaki uniform and "Crikey!" as the style of the late Steve Irwin, Australia's fearless "Crocodile Hunter." Irwin's dangerous encounters with crocodiles and other critters brought the world closer to the wild outdoors, and he became one of the most famous TV personalities in the world.

Irwin's adventures began when he was barely out of diapers. At just four years old, he stepped on a massive, venomous snake and came away unharmed. At age nine, Steve wrestled his first crocodile. He didn't have to be furtive about his animal adventures because his parents shared his passion for wildlife. When Steve was ten, his family bought some land and established a wildlife park that eventually grew into the 60-acre expanse known today as the Australia Zoo.

Later Steve left the park to travel through the Australian wilderness. He captured crocodiles that locals would have otherwise killed. He ameliorated the crocodiles' situation by letting them live in his family's wildlife park.

The "Crocodile Hunter" came to life when Steve and his wife traveled into Australia's mangrove swamps during their honeymoon. Steve's wife videotaped his wrestling matches with crocodiles, and they sold the footage to the Discovery Channel. This video became the first episode of his wildly popular show.

Steve became a celebrity, but he never stopped working for wildlife efforts in Australia and elsewhere. Even after Steve Irwin's death in September 2006, his work continues to motivate people to protect the animals and wild places that he loved.

BEHIND the Lens

Wildlife filmmaker Alex Livingston may not wrestle crocodiles, but he's captured animals from cheetahs to cobras on videotape. We caught up with him between films.

Q: How do you get animals to act the way you want them to in front of the camera?

AL: We don't. They are "wild" animals—they'll tolerate our presence, but we can't hand them scripts and give orders. If we're really stuck, we can put out treats to attract animals, but we never harm animals for the sake of the film.

Q: So how can you create the "stories" of certain animals or places?

AL: With a little creativity. No good filmmaker deceives the audience, but footage can be arranged in a way that gives it a storyline. If a lioness gets tired and capitulates while we're filming, we complete the film at another time using the same animal.

Q: What dangers do you face when filming?

AL: You name it, we face it. Hostile animals, hostile environments, diseases, volcanoes, frostbite, and worse. My worst experience was being stricken with malaria.

Q: What's the most exciting thing you've ever filmed?

AL: In Tanzania, I filmed a cheetah chasing a gazelle at almost 70 miles per hour—incredible!

Rev Up Your Writing

You've just read about people who've been up close and personal with wild animals. What's the wildest wildlife moment you've ever seen on TV? What made this particular moment stand out in your mind? Use as many of the vocabulary words as possible but make sense.

Word Organizer

Copy this graphic organizer onto a separate piece of paper.

List words that mean almost the same as *furtive* and write your answers in the web. Then tell about a time when you saw someone acting furtively.

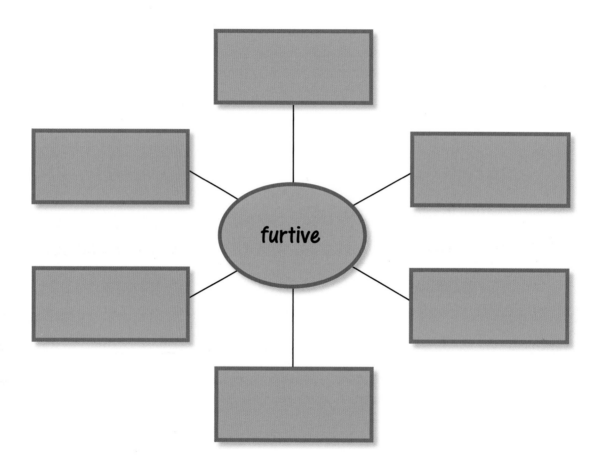

EXTREME

Ocean Shark TOURS

Swimming with the Sharks Since 1993

Want to get nose-to-nose with the planet's most awesome predators? Extreme Ocean Shark Tours will take you there!

Ride with us into the turquoise water off Oahu's North Shore for some serious shark-sighting action. We've never seen fewer than 5 sharks in a day, and our record is 35!

Not only will you see sharks in these waters—humpback whales, dolphins, and sea turtles also reside here. Hop into the shark cage, and if you're lucky, you can stare down a great white shark!

Worried about a shark attack? Don't be. Sharks normally attack when retaliating against an attacker or when they mistake a person for a fish. We possess the most secure shark cages in the world.

WHERE
Coconut Beach, Oahu, Hawaii

WHEN
Every day, unless there is torrential rain!

HOW LONG
Choose a full day, weekend, or one-week tour!

HOW MUCH
Day Trips: $200
Weekend Getaways: $900
One-Week Expeditions: $2,000

We supply your dive gear, meals, and a single-use waterproof camera; the only thing you need to bring is some curiosity and a whole lot of courage.

Take the plunge and swim with us at Extreme Ocean Shark Tours!

An Eco-rific Trip

By Sarah Clapton

I'm not a "nature person," so when I arrived at the Amazonia Ecolodge in Bolivia, I wasn't eager to learn about the Amazon rain forest. I was more concerned about whether I'd have to share my sleeping bag with giant bugs. In fact, I was so preoccupied with my fears that I nearly missed the flock of macaws perched on the lodge roof. But when I noticed them, I stared, rapt, at the blue and gold birds. I was deep in the Amazon, surrounded by a silver lake, emerald rain forest, and hundreds of unusual creatures.

My worries over insects dissolved once I saw my cabin—a wooden cottage tucked back in the rain forest, complete with a hammock stretched across the porch. And inside? A soft bed covered with mosquito netting. Perfect.

I also loved the resort's forest tours that explain the many uses of rain forest plants. We took boat trips across a beautiful lake and saw lots of wildlife: bright blue frogs, yellow-billed toucans, and more!

Most importantly, all of the Ecolodge's profits go to maintaining and protecting the endangered rain forests of Bolivia. It's a long way from home, but Amazonia Ecolodge is worth the visit!

Rev Up Your Writing

You've just read ads for some exciting vacation destinations. If you could take any kind of vacation, where would you go? Write about your dream vacation. Use as many of the vocabulary words as possible but make sense.

Can You Relate?

Copy this graphic organizer onto a separate piece of paper. Match the following words with their related vocabulary word. If a word relates to more than one vocabulary word, explain why.

absolution If you give someone absolution, you forgive him or her.

begrudge If you do something begrudgingly, you do it even though you don't want to.

gratify If you try to gratify someone, you try to please that person.

redress If you redress something, you try to make things right for a person who was wronged.

retribution If you get retribution for something that was done to you, you get revenge.

ameliorate	capitulate	retaliate

LESSON 2
DAY
9

In Your Own Words

Respond to one of the following prompts on a separate piece of paper. As you respond, use as many of the vocabulary words as possible. Be creative but make sense!

▶ Write about a time when you or someone you know discovered something amazing on a vacation or long trip. Describe why it was so important and how it changed their or your life.

▶ Write a short story about a family vacation that turns into a wilderness adventure.

▶ Write about a topic of your choice.

VOCABULARY

stricken
torrent
rapt
preoccupied
possess
expanse
retaliate
ameliorate
capitulate
furtive

My Dad, the KING of Cool

By Carlos Sanchez
Illustrated by Tom McNeely

How much can an air conditioner teach you about life? In this biography the writer examines the life of his father, an air conditioner mechanic who passed down important skills—along with valuable wisdom.

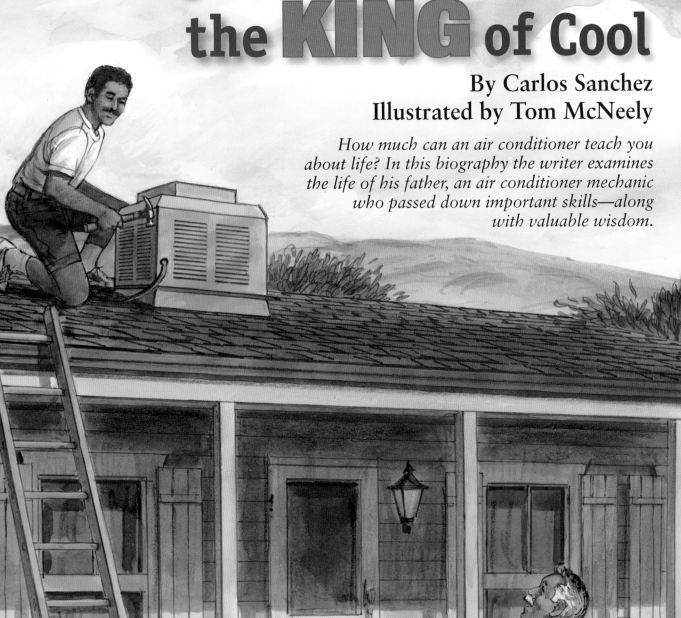

Today marks the first time in 84 years that my father, Jose Angel Sanchez, hasn't celebrated his birthday. He died in May. Unfortunately, it was one of those slow, lingering deaths—the last vestiges[1] of a decades-long battle with Parkinson's disease.[2]

As I mourn his loss, however, I can't help but smile because of those things he'll always represent to me. There's love and strength. Lots of humor. But mostly my father represents air conditioning. In fact, when I rushed home to El Paso in May and learned that he was all but certain to die, I did what came naturally to me: I climbed the roof of my parent's home, the home I grew up in, and began working on my father's air conditioner.

There are men I know who shared sports with their fathers. There are men, such as my older brother, who shared politics. My dad and I shared air conditioning.

Not those bulky, impersonal refrigerated units that are a mainstay in Central Texas homes. I'm talking swamp coolers: mechanical works of art that can stir the senses. They're the workhorses[3] of desert towns such as El Paso where the air is dry and the summer sun bakes its inhabitants; unlike the steaming that Austin weather provides.

These ingenious devices work on the same principle as a desert rainfall: Throw cool moisture in the air and the temperature drops. In swamp coolers, the air is moistened after it passes through wet straw pads and is then forced down a vent into the house by a giant blower. It's not only a cool air that caresses your skin, but a scented air that smells as good as a desert rainstorm.

My personal odyssey with air conditioning was the direct result of my dad being an air-conditioning mechanic. He learned his craft in the Army during World War II.

In my house, preparing the swamp cooler for summer was an art form. Often when we were invited to the roofs of neighbors or relatives seeking my father's expertise, he would delight in pointing out what was wrong with the air conditioner.

FOOTNOTES

[1] *vestiges:* traces or remains
[2] *Parkinson's disease:* a disease that affects a person's ability to use his or her limbs
[3] *workhorse:* person or thing that is strong and reliable

I imagine it was the same type of delight that sports fathers took in predicting that the next pitch would be a curveball.

Before he ever touched the unit, he could look at a small copper tube that feeds water from a line through the house to the swamp cooler and predict that there would be a leak in it and why. It was hot, grueling work that involved scouring down the air conditioner with a wire brush. There was a definite hierarchy. My father handled the plumbing and electrical work while my brother and I cleaned. And cleaned. And cleaned.

Years later, and now that I'm the father of my own two sons, my dad's motives became more clear: He was mostly occupying our time with mindless chores while he did the important work. But in my young mind, I was integral to the process.

Toward that end, I demanded to learn more. I constantly pestered my father about letting me use the wrench to connect the water line or letting me spray paint. And every year, to my immense satisfaction, he let me do more. (I have been doing much the same thing with my eldest son, who still thinks it's cool to use the lawn mower.)

But this was not simply a lesson in mechanics. I learned about life on top of the roof. My father was a gifted storyteller, and he regaled me with stories of his youth in Seguin.[4]

My favorite involved the story of his father's hammer: He grew up near the Guadalupe River, and they fished off a small pier there. As a youth, my dad got it in his mind that he was going to borrow his father's hammer and go underwater to fix a loose leg of the pier. But his father refused to lend him the hammer, saying that he would lose it. And, just like I would have done, my father borrowed the hammer anyway and dove into the water to fix that pier. Only he got his trunks caught on an exposed root of a pecan tree and in his struggle to save his life, he lost the hammer in the river muck and ripped off his suit.

How true that story is I'll never know. What I do know is that to this day, I treat my father's tools as gold.

I learned about other things on top of our roof. . . . And it was up there that I learned politics.

FOOTNOTES
••••••••••••••••••••••
[4] *Seguin:* a city in south central Texas

During the annual air-conditioning ritual, I first heard the story of Felix Longoria, the Texan from Three Rivers who died in combat in World War II only to be denied a funeral in his hometown because he was Mexican. Lyndon Johnson[5] stepped in, as my father told it, and arranged for Longoria to be buried at Arlington National Cemetery[6] with full military honors. There was a rare reverence in his voice as he told that story—not only for Longoria, whom my dad considered a hero, but for LBJ,[7] who did right by my dad.

My father's heroes became my heroes. But of course my biggest hero was my father.

And there was nothing more heroic than that moment of truth when it was time to turn on the air conditioner. With the unit assembled and gleaming, my father would descend the ladder and go inside. He would close all the vents in the house and leave a single one open, covering it with a wet towel. Then, with a ceremonial flip of a switch, the air would blow in, the wet towel catching any dust. My family all stood beneath the vent as part of this ceremony. And with almost the reverence of watching someone retire the American flag, we watched as my father lowered the towel to allow the cool air to rush into the house.

Nothing delighted me more than hearing someone, my mother typically, soon complain that it was too cold in the house.

As the years went on, the annual ritual became less frequent. After I left home at age 18, the ritual became virtually nonexistent. But I always felt a sense of duty whenever I visited in the early spring. If I was in town, I would always help my father fix the air conditioner.

It was up there on that roof that I first witnessed the slight tremor in his hand that I came to know as Parkinson's, the neurological[8] disease that eventually would debilitate him. As the disease progressed, my father would stand in the yard with his walker, yelling at me up on the roof, guiding me through the ritual. Several springs later, he did his yelling from a wheelchair.

Still it came as a surprise to me this spring—as my father lay dying in a hospital bed and I climbed on the roof to fix the air conditioner—that I realized I had set out to complete the ritual for the first time in my life without my father's help.

I stood atop the roof with an initial sense of sadness. As I panned the reaches of my old neighborhood, everything looked much more aged than I remember. I walked slowly to the swamp cooler and gave it a visual inspection.

Looking down at the copper tube that brings water from the house to the cooler, as if by second nature, I shook my head thinking to myself that someone had improperly disconnected it last year.

And just as my father had done for so many springs in my life, I predicted where that copper tubing would leak. I turned on the flow of water and, with a mixture of pride and sorrow, I sat down on the roof, water spewing from the leaking pipe. Then I said goodbye to my father.

Explain Yourself

Answer each question on a separate piece of paper. Be sure to explain your answers.

1. Would you make broccoli the **mainstay** of your diet? Why or why not?

2. Describe an **odyssey** that you would like to go on.

3. Would a lazy person enjoy **grueling** work? Why or why not?

4. What would you use to **scour** a window? Explain.

5. Would you expect to find a **hierarchy** on a football team? Explain.

6. Is a microwave an **integral** part of a kitchen? Explain.

7. Would you want to **regale** someone you did not like? Why or why not?

8. Why would you **pan** the school cafeteria after getting your lunch? Explain.

9. Does an Olympic athlete deserve to be treated with **deference**? Explain.

10. Would you consider a CD player to be the **epitome** of all audio listening devices? Why or why not?

VOCABULARY

mainstay A mainstay is the most important part of something, the part that supports everything else.

odyssey An odyssey is a long, eventful journey.

grueling A grueling experience is so difficult it exhausts you.

scour When you scour something, you scrub it in order to clean it.

hierarchy A hierarchy is a way of ranking group members based on their importance.

integral Something that is an integral part of something else is absolutely necessary for it to work.

regale If you regale someone, you entertain him or her with stories.

pan If you pan an area, you look slowly across it from side to side.

deference When you show deference, you act in a way that shows a deep respect for someone or something.

epitome The epitome of something is the best example or model of it.

Take It Further

Complete these sentences on a separate piece of paper.

1. Once I started middle school, the **mainstay** of my social life became . . .

2. The explorer's **odyssey** was amazing because . . .

3. Learning to swim can be **grueling** if . . .

4. Marco **scoured** his motorcycle after . . .

5. At the top of my school's social **hierarchy** are the . . .

6. I believe exercise is **integral**, so I . . .

7. Kim Nguyen, a professional basketball player, **regaled** us with . . .

8. Before Kerry began her presentation, she **panned** the audience to . . .

9. Sheila felt it was important to show **deference** to . . .

10. Abdul thought the **epitome** of rock music was . . .

Explore It

Did you know that many of the words and expressions that we use every day are related to ships and sailing? The word *mainstay*, for example, refers to the rope that supports the mast of a sailing ship. The mainstay is needed for a ship to sail. So, we use the word *mainstay* to describe the most important part of something.

Work with a partner to provide a brief explanation of how the phrases in the left column are used, and match each phrase to the correct nautical description. Be prepared to share your answers.

1. under the weather	A. to be familiar with the hundreds of feet of ropes in a square rigged ship
2. to the bitter end	B. the last signal given by a ship officer that meant "lights out" and "silence"
3. to know the ropes	C. the end of an anchor cable; in bad weather, it was reached
4. pipe down	D. an area below the deck where the movement of the ship is less noticeable

Significant

JuNk

W hat do worn-out shoes, broken toys, and a 1955 bus have in common? Such random items are integral pieces of Tyree Guyton's Heidelberg Project. Located on Heidelberg Street in Detroit, Michigan, the Heidelberg Project is an outdoor exhibit of abandoned houses, cars, and other fixtures that Guyton decorated with found objects and brightly-colored polka dots.

Since the late 1980s, Guyton's bizarre efforts have helped lessen crime in the surrounding neighborhood by drawing attention to areas where criminals liked to prowl. When the outside of the first house was decorated with polka dots, toys, a dog house, and other objects, people passing through the area immediately took notice. As more and more people began to pay attention to the house and the surrounding area, criminals and lawbreakers were scared away. Thus, Guyton's artwork became a meaningful and effective way to bring people of all ages together while driving out crime.

Despite the positive effects of the Heidelberg Project, a number of people in Detroit felt the houses were eyesores. These people succeeded in having a few of the houses destroyed. However, many more people thought the Heidelberg Project was the epitome of junk art. In the last 20 years, visitors from at least 89 countries have visited the outdoor art display to show deference for both the art and the artist.

Tyree Guyton's odyssey with art has taken him around the world. In addition to appearing on talk shows and in magazines, he has regaled millions of people with stories about his life experiences and unique talents.

Make Your Own Junk ART

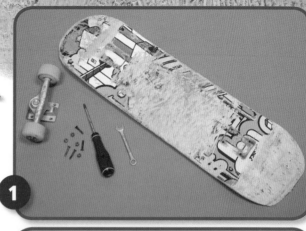

Junk art is all about being creative with everyday materials. Even though you can buy things for your art project, most of the fun comes from trying to find weird stuff to include in your wacky work of art. Here's one way to make fantastic junk art by combining an old skateboard and chalkboard.

1 Find something to use as a basis for your art project and prepare it for decoration.
  - If you're using an old skateboard, be sure to take the wheels off first.

2 Create a message board with a small chalkboard.
  - If you don't have a chalkboard, buy chalkboard paint at a hardware store.
  - Decorate the chalkboard, and hang chalk from it.

3 Decorate your creation.
  - Search your house for old toys or broken-down parts from an old bicycle or radio.

Make sure that your junk art doesn't include priceless family valuables—get permission before you use something for your art. With some glue, scissors and a little imagination, you'll regale your friends with the coolest message board of all time!

Rev Up Your Writing

You've just read about ways to find creative value in everyday objects. Write about a time when you found a creative or unusual use for an object or saw an object around you being put to creative use. Use as many of the vocabulary words as possible but make sense.

Word Organizer

Copy this graphic organizer onto a separate piece of paper.

Scour is at the hot end of the Word-O-Meter. Think of words that would be colder. Write your answers in the boxes. Explain your answers.

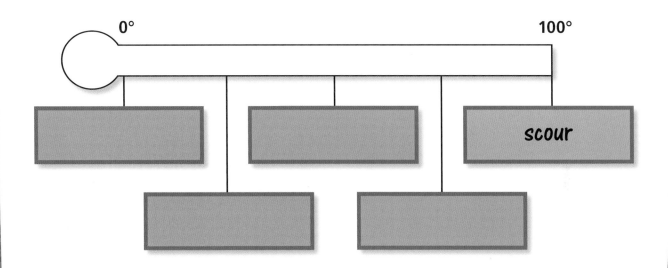

0°   100°

scour

Did You Know?

A giraffe can scour its ears with its own tongue.

43

SMALL WONDERS

You have probably heard the term "bigger is better." But in many cases, the smaller the size of something, the more amazing it is. Whether they are used for medicine or art, these tiny marvels are creating a big uproar.

Mini Medical Helpers

Imagine a robot that can jump over organs and crawl under veins. Think it sounds like science fiction? Actually, it's science fact! Scientists at research facilities across the country are developing microscopic robots that can scour delicate blood vessels and travel through organs to destroy deadly tumors. These mini medics might become the mainstay of future medicine.

Giant Panda— on a strand of hair?

Micro-painter Jin Yin Hua uses a single rabbit hair like a tiny brush to paint animals, famous celebrities, and presidents on thin strands of human hair. It takes him over a week to create just one of these miniature masterpieces. Talk about a grueling way to paint!

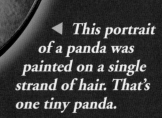

◄ *This portrait of a panda was painted on a single strand of hair. That's one tiny panda.*

▲ Sculpture of a
tiger in the eye
of a needle.

Willard's Whimsy

If you look through the eye of a needle,
what do you see? Not much, right? Well,
if you use a microscope to pan the eye of
a needle from a Willard Wigan Exhibition,
you might see the Statue of Liberty, a barn
owl, a string quartet, or even an adorable baby.
Willard Wigan, a resident of Birmingham, England,
is a micro-sculptor. He molds specks of minerals,
dust, spider webbing, and paint into highly detailed
sculptures that can fit within the eye of a sewing
needle and other tiny places. While other artists
have made micro art, Wigan is surely at the top
of the hierarchy!

◄ Although the
sculpture may
look gigantic,
this replica of the
Statue of Liberty
was actually made
in the eye of a
needle.

Rev Up Your Writing

You've just read about the challenging
task of working with microscopic
objects. Artists and scientists do so
every day—perhaps for the love of
the finished product. Write about a
challenging task you do or have done
that you find rewarding. Use as many
of the vocabulary words as possible
but make sense.

Can You Relate?

Copy this graphic organizer onto a separate piece of paper. Match the following words with their related vocabulary word. If a word relates to several vocabulary words, explain why.

indefatigable People who are indefatigable never get tired.
mettle Someone who has mettle is brave and courageous.
paragon If you say that someone is a paragon of something, you mean that he or she is a perfect example of it.
pinnacle When you reach the pinnacle of something, you reach its highest point.
upright An upright person is honest.

deference	odyssey	epitome

In Your Own Words

Respond to one of the following prompts on a separate piece of paper. As you respond, use as many of the vocabulary words as possible. Be creative but make sense!

▶ Have you ever heard the saying, "One person's trash is another person's treasure?" Write about something you own that is important to you but that someone else would throw away. Why is this object so important to you?

▶ Willard Wigan's fascination with small things began when he was a child. Write a brief essay about any hobbies or interests from your childhood that you continue to do today.

▶ Write about a topic of your choice.

VOCABULARY

mainstay
odyssey
grueling
scour
hierarchy
integral
regale
pan
deference
epitome

A Picture of
My Mother's Family

By Wing Tek Lum • Illustrated by Lin Wang

*How much can a picture really tell you about
a family you never knew? That's the question
a poet faces when an old photograph helps
him imagine what life was like for his
mother and her family.*

At a summer home in Ningpo, near Shanghai,[1]
your family (circa 1915) poses on the stone floor entryway
between the rise of steps and the wood front door.
Four girls are spread about the parents,
who are seated. All are in warm clothing,
finely dressed. It is perhaps morning, the coolness
captured now in such clear light: they seem, somehow,
more illumined[2] by beams emanating from the moon.

On the right, Ming, the second-born, my living aunt,
has on a dark wool dress and brocaded[3] top of silk
that does not cover her sleeves. She tiptoes slightly,
for she leans to one side on her hidden right arm
bracing, it would seem, on the edge of her father's chair.
Her face—cocked to her right in front of his chest—
is plump. The supple mouth I recognize
smiles downward, frowning: sad and shy
in her own young world. This photograph is hers;
last year she gave it to me in remembrance of you.

My grandfather is seated on white upholstery,[4]
upright, balding and in black, even to his bow tie.
The shine on his shoes reflects into the camera
as he looks on, disregarding the cluster of children,
towards his right faraway. I imagine a dark rose
has caught his proud eye, though I do not know
if such flowers have ever grown there.
The grain of the picture reveals his fine hands,
as if all were focused upon them alone.
The fingers are brown and slender, recalling
that he was a doctor, and that these are doctor's hands.
Gnarled roots, they had grown as pale as his beard
and clothes, when we saw him—I at the age of five
in Hong Kong, after he was allowed in for the last time.

Holding his right hand in her small clasp,
her arm snuggled against his thigh, the third daughter
(maybe three) glances with eyebrows raised
somewhere in the direction of her father's gaze.
Her stance is as wide as her padded skirt, disclosing
beneath a small foot balancing on its outer side.
I guess that her silk top is red, a color
of wide cherries. The shortest in the picture,
she stands dwarfed by the shadows looming behind her.
Funny, but I don't even know her name; I think
she was the one, you said, who never reached her teens.

Lucy, the youngest sister, leans forward
on her mother's lap: squirming, I assume,
for her left arm is in a blur, swinging,
her mouth opened round, voicing her discomfort.
She is all white in a doll's bonnet and long dress,
as if she were attending her own wedding.
More likely, it's her birthday . . .
She never married, moved to Chicago near Ming.
At forty, she visited our home, skinny and sallow
from cancer. Soon after, picking me up
from school, you told me, "she just passed away."

Caught at that moment, your mother looks into the lens,
while restraining her daughter: her hands in front
encircling the waist. She wears a wan smile,
almost serene. Partly it's because of her face,
which seems flat. I can discern no part of her nose,
except for the line of a shadow beneath her nostrils.
Her trousers are nearly covered by the spread
of Lucy's dress. I notice that wrinkles have begun
to set under her eyes; they make her appear
out of focus, like crying. I muse about
whether her feet were bound.[5] A pastor's daughter,
she died young. My grandfather remarried.

FOOTNOTES

[5] *feet were bound:* an outdated Chinese practice of tightly wrapping girls' feet to make them smaller

The one on the left end, you are as tall
as your parents are when seated. With black boots on
you balance playfully on the balls of your feet,
a bit pigeon-toed.[6] For you, the oldest,
your mother has combed all your hair back tightly
about your head; you wear to one side a paper flower:
white, to match your own long blouse and pants.
Although proper, I suppose, the sleeves
and the trouser legs are cut three-quarters length,
as if you had already outgrown these clothes.
Forearms exposed, I can see a thin bracelet
around each wrist. With your flat nose
and flower, I almost think you are a small clown.
Your mouth closed, you keep smiling straight at me.

FOOTNOTES
....
[6] *pigeon-toed:* with the
toes turned inward

Explain Yourself

Answer each question on a separate piece of paper. Be sure to explain your answers.

1. Would you want to ride on a **supple** skateboard? Why or why not?

2. Would you ever **disregard** a phone message from a friend? Explain.

3. Do you think the roots of a 2-year-old tree would be **gnarled**? Why or why not?

4. When was the last time you looked **wan**? Explain.

5. What might you and your friends **muse** about? Explain.

6. If you were cooking dinner, would you want **explicit** directions to follow? Why or why not?

7. What television shows make you feel **nostalgic**? Explain.

8. What movie would you watch if you felt **somber**? Why?

9. Where do teenagers like to **congregate**? Explain.

10. Would you **postulate** that most 18-year-olds vote? Why or why not?

supple   Something that is supple is soft and bends easily.

disregard   If you disregard something, you decide it is not worth paying attention to.

gnarled   Something that is gnarled is wrinkled and twisted, usually because it is old.

wan   People who look wan look pale because they are weak or worn out.

muse   When you muse about something, you think about it deeply.

explicit   Something that is explicit is explained so clearly that it can't possibly be misunderstood.

nostalgic   When you feel nostalgic, you remember a happier time in the past.

somber   When you are somber, you feel sad and gloomy.

congregate   When people congregate, they come together in a group.

postulate   When you postulate something, you make an educated guess that it is true.

Take It Further

Complete these sentences on a separate piece of paper.

1. When I told my teacher I had invented a **supple** spatula, he . . .

2. When choosing what to wear for the prom, you shouldn't **disregard** . . .

3. On our camping trip, we saw a **gnarled** . . .

4. They all looked **wan** after a day of . . .

5. As Trina flipped through the magazine, she **mused** about . . .

6. The map Gwen drew was so **explicit** that . . .

7. Gertrude gets **nostalgic** when she . . .

8. Our class was **somber** when we heard . . .

9. We **congregated** in Billy's room because . . .

10. After looking at all the data, Sheila **postulated** that . . .

Explore It

Everyone knows about the silent letters in words like *know* and *crumb*, but some silent letters appear less often, like the *g* at the beginning of *gnarled*.

Working with a partner or small group, research other words that have a silent *g*. Once you have discovered four or more of them, create and perform a skit using all of the words. Make it as exciting as you can but be sure to use the words correctly!

Keeping an Eye on Technology

Some researchers think that we'll soon be able to get rid of the mouse for good! Don't worry, animal lovers; I'm not talking about the furry kind. I'm talking about that little piece of computer equipment with the gnarled old cord.

Scientists are currently working on technologies that will let you use your eyes as your mouse. You'll be able to move a cursor across a screen simply by moving your eyes. Video game victories will no longer depend so much on supple fingers and quick reflexes; instead, you'll control games with your eye movements!

The technology is still being researched, but it looks promising. Scientists like Professor Guang-Zhong Yang have been studying how the brain reacts when you recognize something with your eyes. Although they don't have an explicit understanding of that process yet, researchers' discoveries will help them re-create it with computer technology.

Advertisers might use the technology to track viewers' responses to commercials and Web pages. It might also be used to design a safety system that could alert drivers who start to fall asleep at the wheel. Scientists even believe that fighter pilots might one day aim missiles by looking at their targets. When it comes to eye-tracking technology, the eye's the limit!

Your Biology is the Key

Researchers at security companies are always looking for unique ways to make keys to their locks. Some security companies now make safes that rely on fingerprints. The safes have computer programs that memorize the owner's fingerprints. The safe will open only when the owner presses his or her fingertips to the sensor. Similarly, some companies have developed fingerprint sensors for use in cars. Car owners scan and register their fingerprints. To start the car, the owner places a finger on the scanner. This new technology might make criminals nostalgic for the days when they could "hotwire" a car.

Does a long wait in the cafeteria lunch line leave you wan and impatient? Soon that wait could be shorter. About 800 school districts in the United States plan to introduce voice-recognition systems in their lunchrooms. To order lunch, students will simply say their name, student number, and order. Their account information will appear on the food server's computer screen, and families will be billed automatically for the meals!

Rev Up Your Writing

You've just read about some amazing new inventions that could make everyday tasks a lot simpler. Write about something that you'd like to improve. What could you invent to help improve it? Describe how the invention would look and work. Use as many of the vocabulary words as possible but make sense.

Word Organizer

Copy this graphic organizer onto a separate piece of paper.

Think of words that describe things that are supple and write your answers in the ovals. Then give examples of things that are supple and write your answers in the boxes. Explain your answers.

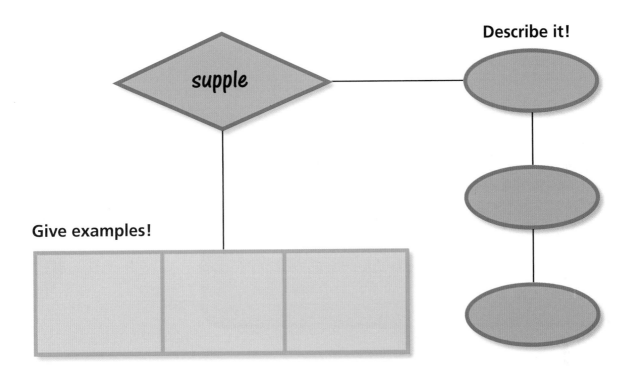

Describe it!

supple

Give examples!

Antarctica:
Fact or Fiction?

FACT or FICTION?

When people in Antarctica talk about "growlers," they're talking about polar bears.

FICTION! Polar bears live in the Arctic, not the Antarctic. A growler is an iceberg that's hard to see because it's partially covered by water.

FACT or FICTION?

Antarctica is the largest desert in the world.

FACT! As you muse about deserts, remember that they are not always hot. Even though Antarctica has snow, the amount of snow that falls there each year is so small that Antarctica is technically considered a desert.

FACT or FICTION?

No humans live in Antarctica.

FICTION! Scientists from around the world live in special stations in Antarctica so they can do research there. Not all residents of Antarctica are scientists, though. Some are workers who take care of the Antarctic buildings, and at least one baby has been born there!

FACT or FICTION?

Scientists congregate in Antarctica to look for meteors.

FACT! Antarctica is covered in clean white snow. The snow makes it difficult to disregard any dark-colored meteors that fall to Earth from space. Some of the meteors in Antarctica are pieces of Mars!

FACT or FICTION?

Antarctica is the highest, driest, coldest, windiest, and darkest continent.

FACT & FICTION! Antarctica is higher, drier, colder, and windier than any other continent on earth. However, the skies are dark and somber for only part of the year. Although the sun never rises in Antarctica in the winter, it never sets there during the summer!

FACT or FICTION?

Antarctica contains 90 percent of the world's ice.

FACT! Scientists postulate that Antarctica has about seven million cubic miles of ice.

Rev Up Your Writing

People have lots of ideas about what Antarctica is like, but their ideas aren't always correct. Write about a time when you realized that your ideas about something weren't entirely true. What made you change your mind? Use as many vocabulary words as possible but make sense.

Can You Relate?

Copy this graphic organizer onto a separate piece of paper. Match the following words with their related vocabulary word. If a word relates to more than one vocabulary word, explain why.

extrapolate   If you extrapolate, you make a prediction based on things you already know.

pensive   A pensive person thinks deeply and seriously about things.

poignant   A poignant story affects the reader's emotions.

premeditated   Something premeditated is thought about and planned in advance.

ruminate   When you ruminate about something, you think about it for a long time.

muse	somber	postulate

In Your Own Words

VOCABULARY

supple
disregard
gnarled
wan
muse
explicit
nostalgic
somber
congregate
postulate

Respond to one of the following prompts on a separate piece of paper. As you respond, use as many of the vocabulary words as possible. Be creative but make sense!

▶ Write about a time when you or someone you know went on a trip to a strange or unfamiliar place. Was the experience exciting, scary, or both? How was the place similar to your home? How was it different?

▶ Write a poem about one or two people in your family. Draw your readers into the poem by using vivid descriptions and language that expresses your emotions.

▶ Write about a topic of your choice.

The Tale of the Falcon

By Giovanni Boccaccio
Retold by Kalina Chausovsky
Illustrated by Joel Spector

Federigo has spent most of his life trying to win Monna's heart, but all of his attempts fail miserably. Will Federigo be able to help Monna when she needs him the most?

*T*here once was a young man named Federigo. He lived in Florence,[1] was very wealthy, and was in love with a beautiful woman, Monna Giovanna. The only problem was that she was not in love with him.

Federigo tried desperately to win Monna's affections. He hosted huge parties and feasts and participated in jousting[2] tournaments, all in her honor. He spent his money freely, doing everything he could think of to attract Monna's attention. Unfortunately, none of it worked. Monna wasn't impressed by large, ornate[3] displays of affection, and the more Federigo tried to impress her, the more he pushed her away.

Well, as will happen when you are spending money faster than you are making it, Federigo lost his fortune. Defeated, he took his only remaining property, a falcon, to his small farm in the countryside. There he spent his time tending his farm and hawking;[4] he asked nothing of anybody, and quietly tolerated his poverty.

During this time, Monna Giovanna married and had a son. They lived blissfully in the city until her husband fell ill and died. Even though her husband had left her and her son a considerable fortune and they could have afforded to stay in the city, she could not bear to be surrounded by the life they had built together; Monna and her son moved out to the countryside, not too far from Federigo's small farm.

In the months that followed, Monna's son became friends with Federigo. The young boy had never seen anything like Federigo's falcon and would talk of the bird's strength and agility for days after hawking excursions. At night, he dreamed the bird was actually his own, but he didn't dare ask Federigo for it. He knew the falcon was the only thing of worth his friend had left.

During this time Monna's son became ill. Having already lost her husband, Monna was terrified her son would die. She spent every waking minute by his bedside, wiping his feverish face with a wet cloth and asking if there was anything, anything at all, the boy needed or desired. After many days of hearing his mother ask if there was anything he wanted, the young boy finally broke down and confessed:

"Mother, if you could do just one thing for me, please go to Federigo and ask if I may have his falcon. I know that if I could have it, I would be so happy I would be sure to get better."

FOOTNOTES

[1] *Florence:* a city in Italy

[2] *jousting:* a sport in which riders on horseback charge each other and try to knock each other off their horses with long poles

[3] *ornate:* very fancy and elaborate

[4] *hawking:* using a trained hawk to hunt for other birds

At this Monna was struck silent. She knew what the falcon meant to Federigo, a man who had lost all he had in his attempts to win her heart. How could she possibly go and take the only thing he had left? But then she looked at her son, pale and sick, and saw the hope burning in his eyes. She could not tell him no.

"Rest easy. Tomorrow morning I will go to Federigo and convince him to give me the falcon."

At this the boy beamed with delight, and that evening his condition actually seemed to improve. At seeing this turnaround in her son's health, Monna became more determined than ever that what she was going to do the next day was right.

The next morning, Monna left early for Federigo's farm. As she walked, she thought about their past and all the things he had done in his attempts to win her affections. Her heart ached knowing that she was going to him now to take away his most prized possession, but the heartbreak she felt over her son outweighed this ache.

As she came up to his farm, she saw Federigo working in his garden.

"Hello, Federigo," she called.

"My lady," he replied, looking amazed that she was there and embarrassed about the dirt on his clothes. "To what do I owe the honor of your visit?"

"I know that it's a little late, but I have come to apologize for all the suffering I have caused you. I would like to have lunch with you, and I can only hope that it will in some small way compensate for the things I have put you through."

At this, Federigo smiled. "Madam, I cannot think of a single moment when I suffered because of you. On the contrary, you have brought me only happiness and direction. I only wish that I may honor you as much as you deserve."

Monna blushed at this man's steady love and devotion to her, but she remembered her unhappy mission and did not allow herself to feel joy.

Federigo ushered her into his home, and begged her to sit at the window and enjoy the flowers as he rushed to prepare a lunch for her. He knew that the simple vegetables and bread he usually served would not be good enough for her, so he ran madly around the room, looking for something that would do.

And then, his eyes fell on his falcon. It was plump and healthy, and it was the only thing he had that was worthy of serving. He promptly wrung its neck, plucked it, and roasted it. He set the table with the nicest dishes he had, and when all was ready, called Monna in for lunch. They ate the falcon, and Monna complimented Federigo several times on the delicious food.

When lunch was over, Monna knew it was time to reveal the true intent of her visit.

"Federigo, when you hear what I have to ask of you, you will no doubt be amazed at my audacity. To have played such a part in your financial ruin and the course of your life, and then to come and ask anything of you, seems too presumptuous for words. But you have met my son and know what a wonderful, kind boy he is, and if only you could understand a mother's devotion, you might understand why I have come here today. My son has fallen ill, and I fear he may die. He has become so taken with your falcon in the time you and he have gone hawking together. You see, I am here to ask for your falcon. He has asked for it, and I believe the very sight of it will make him better. Do not do this because of the love you feel for me; do it because of the love you feel for my son."

When Federigo heard what Monna was requesting, and knew that he could not give her what she desired since he had just served it to her for lunch, he could not utter a single word. Monna mistook his silence for disbelief at having been asked to give away his falcon, and just as she was about to tell him to forget the whole thing, he spoke.

"My lady, I have often felt that Fate was working against me in this life, never allowing you to love me, causing me to lose my fortune, and now this. You have come to my poor home and asked for a simple gift, a request that my desire to honor you has made impossible to oblige. You see, when you told me you wanted to have lunch with me, I wanted to give you only the very best food, food that I do not have readily at hand in my humble home. But then I remembered my falcon, the very falcon you have just requested. Madam, it is that very falcon you wish to take home to your son that we have just finished eating."

When Monna heard this, she reproached him for killing such a falcon to serve as food, but when she saw what terrible anguish he felt, she thanked him for his devotion to her, which it seemed that no amount of time or poverty could abate. She returned home without the falcon, and, to her great sorrow, her son died a few days later.

After her period of mourning had passed, her brothers began to urge her to marry again; she was still young and now had a fortune to herself.

"If you insist that I marry again, I will marry none other than Federigo degli Alberighi," she declared.

Her brothers, knowing that she had made her mind up and knowing that Federigo was of noble birth, even if he was poor, agreed. The two were married; Federigo managed their finances with much more prudence than he had his own when he was young, and they lived happily together the rest of their days.

Explain Yourself

Answer each question on a separate piece of paper. Be sure to explain your answers.

1. How might you **compensate** your sister after losing her favorite CD?

2. What is something that you have **devotion** for? Explain.

3. Would it be **presumptuous** to go to a party without being invited? Why or why not?

4. What might you **utter** to someone who was feeling upset? Explain.

5. Would you **oblige** a bully? Why or why not?

6. Why might your teacher **reproach** you? Explain.

7. If you twisted your ankle, would you want the pain to **abate**? Why?

8. Would you expect a **prudent** person to make a decision without thinking about it first? Why or why not?

9. Which celebrities are you **enamored** of? Explain.

10. Would you feel **chagrined** after losing a race? Why or why not?

compensate When you compensate someone, you try to make up for something lost or stolen.

devotion Devotion is a deep love and admiration for someone or something.

presumptuous If you are presumptuous, you decide that you have the right to do things that are none of your business.

utter When you utter a word or sound, you say it.

oblige If you oblige someone, you do something for that person because you want to, not because you have to.

reproach When you reproach someone, you criticize that person for doing something wrong.

abate If something abates, it becomes less intense or widespread.

prudence When you show prudence, you plan things carefully and wisely.

enamored When you are enamored with someone, you are fascinated by or in love with that person.

chagrin Chagrin is a feeling of embarrassment because you failed.

Take It Further

Complete these sentences on a separate piece of paper.

1. As **compensation** for forgetting his friend's birthday, Christian . . .

2. Tiara showed her **devotion** to her younger sister when she . . .

3. It was **presumptuous** of Maya to think that she . . .

4. When Calvin heard he was the first place winner, he **uttered** . . .

5. After the waiter overcharged us, he **obliged** us by . . .

6. Theo deserved it when his mother **reproached** him because . . .

7. The rain didn't seem like it was going to **abate**, so we . . .

8. Because I am **prudent** with my money, I . . .

9. Paul became **enamored** with Becky after she . . .

10. I felt **chagrined** after giving my speech because . . .

LESSON 5
DAY
4

Explore It

By now you know the word *utter* means "to say a word or sound," but *utter* can also mean "total and complete." For example, if you wanted to say that a project turned out horribly, you might say it was an "utter failure," but if you wanted to say that your project turned out better than you thought it would, you might say that it was an "utter success."

Working with a partner, write a short story about a band playing at a rock concert. Use both meanings of the word *utter* in your story as many times as you can. Be creative and prepare to share your story with the rest of the class.

What Did You Say?

Ni iru spekti filmon!

Don't feel chagrined if you were unable to understand the sentence above (it means, "Let's go to the movies!"). The phrase looks foreign because it's written in a constructed language called Esperanto. Constructed languages, or conlangs, are made-up languages.

Who invents conlangs?

Sometimes writers develop new languages for characters in books or movies. Author J. R. R. Tolkien is one of the most famous inventors of conlangs. In his *Lord of the Rings* trilogy, Tolkien invented languages such as Quenya and Sindarin. But you don't have to be a famous writer to create a new language. Other people who love working with words have created conlangs, too!

How do people create conlangs?

It takes prudence and patience to create a conlang. It can take years to fully develop a new language. Some people begin by playing around with sounds and words that they enjoy until something catches their attention. For others, the new language begins to develop in their imaginations before it's put down on paper.

Languages of Fiction

Klingon

Klingon, a fictional language invented by Marc Okrand, is spoken by some of the aliens in the Star Trek movies. Unlike English, when capital letters are used in Klingon, they are there to remind you that the letter is uttered differently than it is in English. Klingon is a harsh, raspy language. When speaking Klingon, oblige the people you're speaking to by standing back. That way you won't spray them with saliva!

Quenya

Quenya is one of the fictional languages spoken by elves in the works of J. R. R. Tolkien. It's inspired by Finnish, Latin, and Greek. Because Tolkien only created the phrases and terms needed to use in his novels, Quenya is not a complete language. This has left many people who wish to learn and speak Quenya heartbroken. Some people have tried to compensate for this by developing the language themselves!

Rev Up Your Writing

You've just read about some made-up languages. Suppose you decide to develop your own language. What would your language be like? Write about the language you would create and how you would use it. Use as many of the vocabulary words as possible but make sense.

67

Word Organizer

Copy this graphic organizer onto a separate piece of paper.

List words that mean almost the same thing as *abate* and write your answers in the web.

Then tell about a time when you saw, heard, or felt something abate.

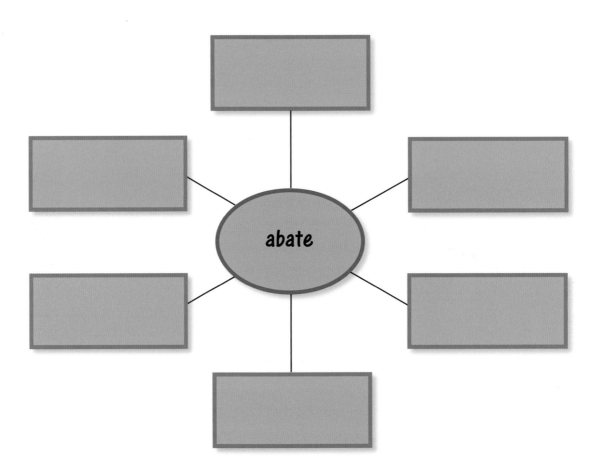

Talking Without Saying a Word

Ask Dr. Jane

Dear Dr. Jane,

I'm very enamored of my girlfriend, Julie. However, her constant fidgeting drives me nuts. She always plays with her hair and bites her nails. And if I ask her a question, she never answers right away. Instead, she tilts her head, then starts stroking her chin or tugging at her ear. What does this mean? Do you think Julie isn't devoted to me?

—Marcus

Dear Marcus,

I don't mean to sound presumptuous, but you need to relax, and so does your girlfriend. It sounds like Julie might be feeling a little insecure. People often stroke their hair or bite their nails when they're nervous. Once you and Julie get more comfortable with each other, her fidgeting should abate.

Don't worry though! Judging from your description of her body language, Julie is definitely interested in you. By tilting her head, she's showing interest in what you have to say. Julie's chin-stroking and ear-pulling habits are also nothing to worry about. People make these gestures when they're trying to decide on something, such as what movie to see or where to go for dinner.

Patience is a virtue,

—Dr. Jane

How Do You Sleep?

When you fall asleep at night, do you curl up on your side, lie on your stomach, or stretch out flat on your back? Chances are, you fall asleep the same way most of the time without even thinking about it. Researchers believe your favorite sleeping position contains hidden clues about your personality.

What does your sleeping position say about you?

I SLEEP . . .

. . . on my stomach with my arms gripping my pillow.

. . . flat on my back with my arms at my sides.

. . . curled up on my side like a baby.

. . . on my side with my arms down.

. . . on my side with my arms in front of me.

WHAT DOES IT MEAN?

You're fearless, outgoing, and even a little outrageous!

You're quiet, and you reproach yourself if you don't live up to your high standards.

Cool and calm on the outside, you're more emotional inside.

You might be shy, but you're quick to lend a helping hand or a sympathetic ear.

You're friendly, but you're not very trusting. You probably think the connection between sleep positions and personality is nonsense!

Rev Up Your Writing

Many people disagree about whether people can actually communicate without saying a word. What do you think? Write about whether you think nonverbal communication is possible and why. Use as many of the vocabulary words as possible but make sense.

Can You Relate?

Copy this graphic organizer onto a separate piece of paper. Match the following words with their related vocabulary word. If a word relates to more than one vocabulary word, explain why.

audacious   Someone who is audacious is bold, daring, and fearless.

culpable   If you are culpable, you are to blame for something that happened.

deprecate   If you deprecate someone, you express your disapproval of him or her.

fiasco   A fiasco is an event that is a complete and total disaster.

lofty   If your behavior is lofty, you are behaving in an arrogant or haughty way.

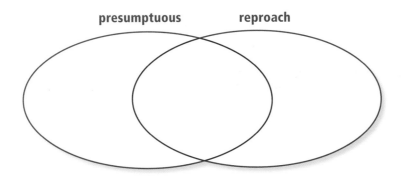

presumptuous   reproach

In Your Own Words

VOCABULARY

compensate
devotion
presumptuous
utter
oblige
reproach
abate
prudence
enamored
chagrin

Respond to one of the following prompts on a separate piece of paper. As you respond, use as many of the vocabulary words as possible. Be creative but make sense!

▶ Write about a time when you or someone you know did something crazy to impress someone. Describe what happened and how the person reacted.

▶ Imagine that you are an expert in nonverbal communication. Write an advice column that helps the students at your school recognize what their actions mean.

▶ Write about a topic of your choice.

My Wild Irish
Rosenblatt

By Roger Rosenblatt
Illustrated by Dom Lee

Roger Rosenblatt doesn't mind his last name, but other people seem to think there's something funny and confusing about it. Will Roger abandon his Rosenblatt? Or will he stand by it proudly and face the consequences?

FROZENWEMM

FROZENWEMM

The name Rosenblatt is the name I was born with, and is the name I write under, and the name used by the people at Reader's Digest sweepstakes when they let me know that I am about to win two houses or $100,000 in cash; but it is not the name by which I think of myself. That name came to me in Ireland in 1965, after twenty-four hard years dealing with Rosenblatt, which is a sonorous[1] name, but unwieldy. There is the *Rosen*, which is musical enough and redolent of flowers. But there is also the *blatt*, which, while merely meaning a leaf or a sheet of paper in German, here has the sound of an overripe pumpkin dropped to the sidewalk from the roof of a cheap hotel.

Yet I lived fairly comfortably with my Rosenblatt throughout childhood, when there were plenty of familial Rosenblatts around me; and I had a grandfather Maximilian Rosenblatt and a grandmother Rose Rosenblatt compared to whose names my own sounded like Cabot. Inevitably there were a few "Rosenfat"s and "Rosenbrat"s hurled by taunting kids. But on the whole, I kind of liked my name, which, for all its weight, had a rather nice roll to it, like Roy Rogers or Robin Roberts, or Robert Redford, who was growing up too.

In teenagehood, however, life got a bit rougher. For one thing, there was a tennis tournament at a private club in Maine that I was not allowed to enter because my name was Rosenblatt. And since my disqualification had less to do with my name than what my name signified,[2] I learned the hard way what's in a name. Then there was a time or two when important people like girls would shiver with giggles at the mere sound of my name. One girl on a beach, with the mellifluous name of Gabrielle, laughed so hard when I said "Rosenblatt," I wanted to tell her I was kidding.

FOOTNOTES

[1] *sonorous:* impressive-sounding

[2] *signified:* meant or symbolized

In college I actually did change my name, on several exam papers, for a whole term—to Roger Craig Lawrence, which I thought had a fine New England gong to it. Professors recognizing my exams by the low grades handed back the papers unerringly without ever saying a word to me, or to my friend Peter Weissman, who changed his name to Peter Scott Douglas. (We had another friend, Bob Lichtenfeld, who changed his name to Van Wyck Klingerman, thus missing the point.) But that was mere collegiate game playing, and I toted old Rosenblatt[3] into graduate school without altering a letter.

There I started to grow happy with my name once again, for by coincidence there were four other Rosenblatts in school at the time, including a Rand Rosenblatt and another Roger, whose existence I discovered when his pals at Princeton wrote to say they were coming to spend the weekend with me. At first the idea of another Roger Rosenblatt was eerie. Dostoevsky and Poe have both written stories about people haunted by exact doubles who bear their names, and do them in. I kept my alter-Roger at a distance. Otherwise I was encouraged by the presence of so many Rosenblatts, whose number provided not only a safety but also a faint sort of pride.

That was short-lived. In adulthood, as I entered it, there were no more taunts and giggles at the name, but there was something as bad, or maybe worse, in the perverse[4] confusion of my name with those that sound like it—the implication being that when you've seen one Rosensomething you've seen them all. And then I went to live in Ireland for a year, where—in spite of the fact that Ireland is the most hospitable country on earth—I encountered the last straw; where my name was so alien, so odd-sounding (as compared with Nic Shiubhlaigh and Gillhooley) that the postman would fake a coughing fit when he said "Good morning," so as not to get past the "Mr."

But his painful courtesy was not what finally persuaded me to change my name. That occurred at a Dublin book auction, the first (and last) I ever attended, where I brought my meager pennies to bid on a small pile of books, which I actually won. "What's the name?" shouted the auctioneer's assistant over the throng. "Rosenblatt," I answered, followed by general murmuring and bewilderment.

"The name, sir?" repeated the assistant.

"Rosenblatt. With two *t's*," as if that were the issue.

"Once more, please?"

FOOTNOTES
3 *toted old Rosenblatt:* carried my name
4 *perverse:* stubborn

"Rosenblatt," said I, loud and clear. And suddenly emboldened, "Rosenblatt" again. And yet another "Rosenblatt," until the full weight of the ancient name, both the Rosen and the blatt, filled the musty hall, thumping on the ceiling, heaving against the walls, the name like a colossus,[5] so big that it extended back in time to Berlin and Heidelberg,[6] to my father and Maximilian and Rose, and all the Rosenblatts forever. I had been challenged in public, and I had risen to it, obliterating all present and former embarrassments, as I, Rosenblatt, stepped forward to claim my pile of books.

There next to the books was a tag on which the assistant had inscribed my name—Frozenwemm. With two *m's*. And I have kept it to this day.

FOOTNOTES
....
[5] *colossus:* enormous or powerful thing
[6] *Berlin and Heidelberg:* cities in Germany

Explain Yourself

Answer each question on a separate piece of paper. Be sure to explain your answers.

1. What musical instruments would you describe as **unwieldy**? Why?

2. Would you enjoy a dinner that is **redolent** of cafeteria food? Explain.

3. How would you react if someone **taunted** you? Why?

4. What are some words that sound **mellifluous** to you? Explain.

5. How would you make the **implication** that your friend talks too much?

6. Would you want to earn a **meager** amount of money? Explain.

7. Why might you need to be **emboldened** at a school dance? Explain.

8. If your softball team **obliterated** the other team, what happened? Explain.

9. Would you try to give an **egregious** performance in a talent show? Why or why not?

10. What could possibly make you feel **abashed**? Explain.

unwieldy   Something that is unwieldy is hard to handle because of its awkward weight or size.

redolent   If something is redolent of something else, it reminds you of that thing.

taunt   A person who taunts you annoys or teases you in order to be hurtful.

mellifluous   Something that sounds mellifluous sounds pleasant and smooth.

implication   An implication is the unspoken meaning or message behind what you say or do.

meager   When there is a meager amount of something, there is very little of it.

embolden   If you feel emboldened by something, you suddenly have the confidence to act boldly and bravely.

obliterate   When you obliterate something, you completely destroy it.

egregious   An egregious act is shockingly bad.

abashed   If you are abashed, you feel ashamed and embarrassed.

Take It Further

Complete these sentences on a separate piece of paper.

1. Carla's skis were so **unwieldy** that . . .

2. Zack thinks freshly baked cookies are **redolent** of . . .

3. Angela **taunted** Jason because . . .

4. Because Maki had such a **mellifluous** voice, . . .

5. The **implication** of Paco's puzzled face was . . .

6. In the desert, there is a **meager** . . .

7. Ali's coach **emboldened** her by . . .

8. Ruby's ant farm was **obliterated** when . . .

9. Tamara made an **egregious** decision to . . .

10. Noel felt **abashed** after he . . .

LESSON 6
DAY
4

Explore It

You know the word *mellifluous,* but did you know that it has a delicious history? The word *mellifluous* actually comes from the Latin words *mellis,* which means "honey," and *fluus,* which means "flow." So, if something is mellifluous, it flows with honey. How is something that sounds mellifluous similar to honey? It's smooth and sweet.

Create your own food-inspired word. First, think of something edible that's special in some way. Add prefixes or suffixes to the name of the food to make your new word. Write a definition for your creation by thinking about the unique qualities of the food you chose. For example, a person who acts rude and sour might behave with *lemonosity.* Someone who's very healthy might be described as *enspinached,* while a person who's *bananaish* is probably quite silly. Use your word in a conversation with your classmates and see if they can guess its definition.

Languages: Lost and Found

You've probably lost many things in your life, but you've probably never lost an entire language.

"Lost languages" are languages that people spoke thousands of years ago that have become obliterated over time. Some linguists, or language experts, don't even know what some languages sounded like or looked like. This makes "finding" lost languages pretty difficult—but it can be done!

For thousands of years, no one could understand an ancient script made of pictures and symbols called Egyptian hieroglyphics. Then, in 1799, French soldiers found a mysterious, unwieldy stone in Rosetta, Egypt. Three different writing systems were carved into the stone: ancient Greek, an old Egyptian script called Demotic, and Egyptian hieroglyphics. Since linguists found that all three texts said the same thing, they used their knowledge of ancient Greek to crack the hieroglyphic code. Thanks to this amazing discovery, the Rosetta stone, and to the linguists, we now know more about the ancient Egyptian language and culture.

Feeling emboldened to explore lost languages for yourself? Check out these mysterious ancient scripts:

~ Maya ~

These complex signs may look like artwork, but they're really symbols of an ancient language. The Central American Maya civilization used a grid of pictures shaped like humans, animals, and other designs to represent the sounds of their language.

~ Meroïtic ~

At first glance, the African Meroïtic script is redolent of Egyptian hieroglyphs, but they're arranged differently and have different meanings. We know what sound each symbol represents, but because no one has spoken the Meroïtic language for 1600 years, we can't understand what those sounds mean.

~ Ogham ~

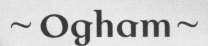

The Ogham script may look like nothing more than a collection of meager lines, but it was used between the third and sixth centuries to write Old Irish. Ogham was often carved into large pieces of stone. Each symbol stands not only for a letter but also for a kind of tree.

Rev Up Your Writing

A language can certainly change over time, and it could become lost forever. Write about changes you've seen in your language. What words do you use that your parents might not understand? How might this change your language in the future? Use as many of the vocabulary words as possible but make sense.

Word Organizer

Copy this graphic organizer onto a separate piece of paper.

Write an explanation of the word *unwieldy* in the Explain It box below. Then write a sentence using the word *unwieldy* in the Use It box. Finally, use the Sketch It box to sketch a picture that shows the word *unwieldy*. Explain your work.

unwieldy **Write It**	**Explain It**
Use It	**Sketch It**

SAY What?!

Have you ever heard someone say something so bizarre that it forced you to pretend to know what he or she was saying, but you really didn't know? Sometimes people make egregious errors, especially when they are trying to sound mellifluous. Avoid endless taunting and always think before you speak!

These people must have felt abashed after saying that!

- I can't reach the brakes on this piano!
- Before I start speaking, I'd like to say something.
- Italics are what Italians write in.

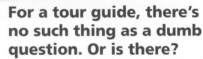

For a tour guide, there's no such thing as a dumb question. Or is there?

- What time does the two o'clock bus leave?
- So what's in the unexplored part of the cave?
- Which beach is closest to the water?
- What is the official language of Alaska?

Oops! Wrong word there!

- Most words are easy to spell once you get the letters write.
- *Don't* is a contraption.
- Good punctuation means not to be late.

81

Newspaper Bloopers

What happens when people twist their words so that they take on new meanings? Check out the headlines and ads in this newspaper. What implications do these headlines make?

Two sisters reunited after 18 years in checkout counter

Enraged cow injures farmer with ax

Miners refuse to work after death

The Daily Blather

Kids Make Nutritious Snacks

Dog for sale: Eats anything and is fond of children.

ve s?

Au_____ Service

Get Rid Of Aunts: Zap does the job in 24 hours.

Dinner Special
Turkey $2.35
Chicken or Beef $2.25
Children $2.00

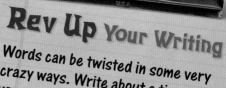

Rev Up Your Writing

Words can be twisted in some very crazy ways. Write about a time when you or someone you know used words creatively. Did you create a pun, write a poem, or accidentally say something silly? Use as many of the vocabulary words as possible but make sense.

Can You Relate?

Copy this graphic organizer onto a separate piece of paper. Match the following words with their related vocabulary word. If a word relates to more than one vocabulary word, explain why.

compunction   Compunction is a feeling of regret for something you've done wrong.

detrimental   If something is detrimental to something else, it causes hurt or damage to it.

diffident   Someone who is diffident is shy and doesn't like to be noticed.

reprehensible   A behavior that is reprehensible is very bad and should be punished.

valor   If you have valor, you have a lot of courage.

embolden	taunt	abashed

In Your Own Words

Respond to one of the following prompts on a separate piece of paper. As you respond, use as many of the vocabulary words as possible. Be creative but make sense!

▶ Write about a time when you met someone who spoke another language or with whom you had a hard time communicating. What problems did you face? Were you able to overcome those problems?

▶ Write an article about your best friend that persuades people to vote for him or her in an upcoming school election. Describe his or her best qualities and tell why people should vote for him or her.

▶ Write about a topic of your choice.

VOCABULARY

unwieldy
redolent
taunt
mellifluous
implication
meager
embolden
obliterate
egregious
abashed

The Anatomy Lesson

By Scott Sanders
Illustrated by Bob Doucet

While studying for an anatomy exam, an eager medical student makes a shocking discovery and uncovers a librarian's terrifying secret.

By the time I reached the anatomy library all the bones had been checked out. Students bent over the wooden boxes everywhere, in hallways and snack bar, assembling feet and arms, scribbling diagrams in notebooks. Half the chairs were occupied by slouching skeletons, and reclining skeletons littered the tables like driftwood. Since I also would be examined on the subject the next day, I asked the librarian to search one last time for bone boxes in the storeroom.

"But I tell you, they've all been given out," she said, glaring at me from beneath an enormous snarl of dark hair, like a fierce animal caught in a bush. How many students had already pestered her for bones this evening?

I persisted. "Haven't you got any damaged skeletons? Irregulars?"

Ignoring my smile, she measured me with her fierce stare, as if estimating the size of box my bones would fill after she had made supper of me. A shadow drooped beneath each of her eyes, permanent sorrow, like the tear mark of a clown. "Irregulars," she repeated, turning away from the counter.

I blinked with relief at her departing back. Only as she slipped noiselessly into the storeroom did I notice her gloved hands. *Fastidious*, I thought. *Doesn't want to soil herself with bone dust and mildew.*

While awaiting my specimens, I studied the vertebrae[1] that knobbed through the bent necks of students all around me, each one laboring over fragments of skeletons. Five lumbar vertebrae,[2] seven cervical,[3] a round dozen thoracic.[4] I rehearsed the names, my confidence building.

Presently the librarian returned with a box. It was the size of an orange crate, wooden, dingy from age or dry rot. The metal clasps that held it shut were tarnished a sickly green. No wonder she wore the gloves.

"This one's for restricted use," she announced, shoving it over the counter.

I hesitated, my hands poised above the crate as if I were testing it for heat.

"Well, do you want it, or don't you?" she said.

FOOTNOTES
[1] *vertebrae:* the bones that make up the spine
[2] *lumbar vertebrae:* the bones in the lower back
[3] *cervical vertebrae:* the bones in the neck area
[4] *thoracic vertebrae:* the bones in the middle of the back

Afraid she would return it to the archives, I pounced on it with one hand and with the other signed the borrower's card. "Old model?" I inquired pleasantly. She did not smile.

I turned away with the box in my arms. The burden seemed lighter than its bulk would have promised, as if the wood had dried with age. Perhaps instead of bones inside there would be pyramids of dust. The metal clasps felt cold against my fingers.

After some searching I found a clear space on the floor beside a scrawny man whose elbows and knees protruded through rents[5] in his clothing like so many lumps of a sea serpent above the waters. When I tugged at the clasps they yielded reluctantly. The hinges opened with a gritty shriek, raising for a moment all round me a dozen glazed eyes, which soon returned to their studies.

Inside I found the usual wooden trays for bones, light as birdwings; but instead of the customary lining of vinyl they were covered with a metal the color of copper and the puttyish consistency of lead. Each bone fitted into its pocket of metal. Without consulting notes, I started confidently on the foot, joining tarsal to metatarsal.[6] But it was soon evident that there were too many bones. Each one seemed a bit odd in shape, with an extra flange[7] where none should be, or a socket at right angles to the orthodox[8] position. The only way of accommodating all the bones was to assemble them into a seven-toed monstrosity, slightly larger than the foot of an adult male, phalanges[9] all of the same length, with ankle-bones bearing the unmistakable nodes[10] for—what? Wings? Flippers?

This drove me back to my anatomy text. But no consulting of diagrams would make sense of this foot. A practiced scrape of my knife blade assured me these were real bones. But from what freakish creature? Feeling vaguely guilty, as if in my ignorance I had given birth to this monstrosity, I looked around the library to see if anyone had noticed. Everywhere living skulls bent studiously over dead ones, ignoring me. Only the librarian seemed to be watching me sidelong, through her tangled hair. I hastily scattered the foot bones to their various compartments.

FOOTNOTES
5 *rents:* rips
6 *tarsal . . . metatarsal:* the bones of the foot
7 *flange:* a projecting rim or edge
8 *orthodox:* usual
9 *phalanges:* toe bones
10 *nodes:* joints

Next I worked at the hand, which boasted six rather than five digits.[11] Two of them were clearly thumbs, opposite in their orientation,[12] and each of the remaining fingers was double-jointed, so that both sides of these vanished hands would have served as palms. At the wrist a socket opened in one direction, a ball joint protruded in the other, as if the hand were meant to snap onto an adjoining one. I now bent secretively over my outrageous skeleton, unwilling to meet stares from other students.

After tinkering with fibula[13] and clavicle,[14] each bone recognizable but slightly awry from the human, I gingerly unpacked the plates of the skull. I had been fearing these bones most of all. Their scattered state was unsettling enough to begin with, since in ordinary skeletal kits they would have been assembled into a braincase. Their gathered state was even more unsettling. They would only go together in one arrangement, yet it appeared so outrageous to me that I forced myself to reassemble the skull three times. There was only one jaw, to be sure, though an exceedingly broad one, and only two holes for ears. But the skull itself was clearly double, as if two heads had been squeezed together, like cherries grown double on one stem. Each hemisphere of the brain enjoyed its own cranium.[15] The opening for the nose was in its accustomed place, as were two of the eyes. But in the center of the vast forehead, like the drain in an empty expanse of bathtub, was the socket for a third eye.

I closed the anatomy text, helpless before this freak. Hunched over to shield it from the gaze of other students, I stared long at that triangle of eyes, and at the twinned craniums that splayed out behind like a fusion of moons. No, I decided, such a creature was not possible. It was a hoax, a malicious joke designed to shatter my understanding of anatomy. But I would not fall for the trick. Angrily I disassembled this counterfeit skeleton, stuffed the bones back into their metal pockets, clasped the box shut, and returned it to the counter.

"This may seem funny to you," I said, "but I have an examination to pass."

"Funny?" the librarian replied.

"This hoax." I slapped the box, raising a puff of dust. When she only lifted an eyebrow mockingly, I insisted, "It's a fabrication, an impossibility."

FOOTNOTES
[11] *digits:* fingers or toes
[12] *orientation:* position
[13] *fibula:* the smaller bone in the lower leg
[14] *clavicle:* collarbone
[15] *cranium:* skull

"Is it?" she taunted, laying her gloved hands atop the crate.

Furious, I said, "It's not even a very good hoax. No one who knows the smallest scrap of anatomy would fall for it."

"Really?" she said, peeling the glove away from one wrist. I wanted to shout at her and then hurry away, before she could uncover that hand. Yet I was mesmerized by the slide of cloth, the pinkish skin emerging. "I found it hard to believe myself, at first," she said, spreading the naked hand before me, palm up. I was relieved to count only five digits. But the fleshy heel was inflamed and swollen, as if the bud of a new thumb was sprouting there.

A scar, I thought feverishly. *Nothing awful.*

Then she turned the hand over and displayed for me another palm. The fingers curled upward, then curled in the reverse direction, forming a cage of fingers on the counter.

I flinched away. Skeletons were shattering in my mind, names of bones were fluttering away like blown leaves. All my carefully gathered knowledge was scattering. Unable to look at her, unwilling to glimpse the socket of flesh that might be opening on her forehead beneath the dangling hair, I kept my gaze turned aside.

"How many of you are there?" I hissed.

"I'm the first, so far as I know. Unless you count our friend here," she added, rapping her knuckles against the bone box.

I guessed the distances to inhabited planets, conjured up the silhouettes of space craft. "But where do you come from?"

"Boise."

"Boise, *Idaho?*"

"Well, actually, I grew up on a beet farm just outside Boise."

"You mean you're—" I pointed one index finger at her and shoved the other against my chest.

"Human? Of course!" She laughed, a quick sound like the release of bubbles underwater. Students at nearby tables gazed up momentarily from their skeletons with bleary eyes. The librarian lowered her voice, until it burbled like whale song. "I'm as human as you are," she murmured.

"But your hands? Your face?"

"Until a few months ago they were just run-of-the-mill human hands." She drew the glove quickly on and touched her swollen cheeks. "My face was skinny. My shoes used to fit."

"Then what happened?"

"I assembled these bones." Again she rapped on the crate. From inside came a hollow clattering, like the sound of gravel sliding.

"You're . . . becoming . . . one of them?"

"So it appears."

Her upturned lips and downturned eyes gave me contradictory messages. The clown-sad eyes seemed too far apart. Even buried under its shrubbery of dark hair, her forehead seemed impossibly broad.

"Aren't you frightened?" I said.

"Not anymore," she answered. "Not since my head began to open."

I winced, recalling the vast skull, pale as porcelain, and the triangle of eyes. I touched the bone box gingerly. "What is it?"

"I don't know yet. But I begin to get glimmerings,[16] begin to see it alive and flying."

"Flying?"

"Swimming, maybe. My vision's still too blurry. For now, I just think of it as a skeleton of the possible, a fossil of the future."

I tried to imagine her ankles affixed with wings, her head swollen like a double moon, her third eye glaring. "And what sort of creature will you be when you're—changed?"

"We'll just have to wait and see, won't we?"

"We?" I echoed, backing carefully over the linoleum.

"You've put the bones together, haven't you?"

I stared at my palms, then turned my hands over to examine the twitching skin where the knuckles should be.

FOOTNOTES
16 *glimmerings:* faint ideas

Explain Yourself

Answer each question on a separate piece of paper. Be sure to explain your answers.

1. Would a **fastidious** person organize his sock drawer? Why or why not?

2. How might a surprise birthday party go **awry**?

3. Would you **gingerly** perform bicycle stunts? Why or why not?

4. How would you feel toward a **malicious** person? Explain.

5. How might you feel if your best friend **mocked** your singing? Explain.

6. Would you buy a gold bracelet that was a **fabrication**? Why or why not?

7. Would you want to **inhabit** Antarctica? Why or why not?

8. What might you **affix** to your backpack? Explain.

9. What would you do if you felt an **incipient** illness? Explain.

10. What would you do if your pet suddenly began to **mutate**?

fastidious   Fastidious people are extremely neat and picky about details.

awry   If something goes awry, it fails to happen in the way it was planned.

gingerly   When you do something gingerly, you do it carefully because you are nervous about making a mistake or getting hurt.

malicious   A malicious person wants to hurt others or cause them pain.

mock   Someone who mocks you imitates you in order to make fun of you.

fabrication   A fabrication is something that is created, not natural.

inhabit   If you inhabit a place, you live there.

affix   When something is affixed, it is attached to something else.

incipient   Something that is incipient is just beginning to happen.

mutate   If something mutates, it changes into some new, usually strange, form.

Take It Further

Complete these sentences on a separate piece of paper.

1. Fatima's classmates thought she was **fastidious** because . . .

2. The awards ceremony went **awry** when . . .

3. Hu moved **gingerly** as he . . .

4. Yuri's **malicious** e-mail caused Zena to . . .

5. While others **mocked** Marlon's speech, Bruce . . .

6. Larry knew the autographed baseball was a **fabrication** when . . .

7. Monroe's family moved to the city and **inhabited** a . . .

8. Yvette tried to **affix** a flower to . . .

9. We could tell the concert was **incipient** because . . .

10. If a fish **mutated**, it might . . .

Explore It

As you now know, when something goes awry, it doesn't turn out as it was planned. The word *awry* comes from the word *wry* which means "twisted, crooked, or bent." *Wry* comes from the Middle English word *wrien* that means "to turn."

Working with a partner, list as many words or phrases as you can that describe a situation that doesn't turn out as planned. Try to come up with expressions you might use with different types of people. For example, when you're telling a friend about a day where everything is going awry, you might say everything is "messed up," but when you tell the principal about the same day, you might say everything "went wrong." Be as creative and funny as you like, and be prepared to share your list with the class.

Smart clothes

If you think technology has nothing to do with fashion, think again!

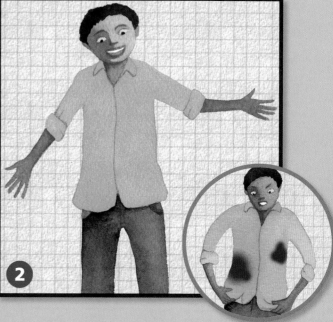

1 Send a hug! No touching required!

Using a combination of emotions and technology, the all-new Huggable Shirt produces a fabrication of your own hug. To send a hug, dial your friend's cell phone and let technology do the rest. The person you're hugging will feel the warmth, pressure, and a heartbeat similar to your own!

2 Stay Ultra Clean

No need to move around gingerly in Ultra Clean casual wear. These clothes are wrinkle-free and stain-proof. From salad dressing to barbecue sauce, Ultra Clean clothing can resist ANY oil- or water-based liquid. The perfect addition to any wardrobe—especially for the not-so-fastidious folks who want to look good without the hassle!

3 What's a girl to do?

A girl wearing Color Mutate clothing simply needs to flip a switch and wait a few moments. Embedded with smart technology, Color Mutate clothing can instantly mutate from its original color and texture to a color and texture of your choice. Simply select the new color and texture on the hidden color dial and go from "blah" to blazing blue, candy apple red, pale pink—the choice is totally yours!

4 The Ultimate Rainwear

Things can go awry if you're caught in the rain without an umbrella—especially if you're already late for a hot date. Now you can waterproof all of your clothes with new Rainwear detergent. Simply add 2 cups to your regular load of laundry. Once your clothes are dry, they will repel water for up to three washes. Buy Rainwear detergent today!

Rev Up Your Writing

You've just read about using technology to improve the use of everyday clothes. What would your outfit of the future look like? Describe your favorite outfit and explain how you would use technology to improve each part of it. Use as many vocabulary words as possible but make sense.

93

Word Organizer

Copy this graphic organizer onto a separate piece of paper.

List words that are synonyms of *fastidious*. Write your answers in the Synonyms box. Use some of the words in this box to describe a fastidious person you know or a fastidious character from a TV show.

Then list words that are antonyms of *fastidious*. Write your answers in the Antonyms box. Use some of the words in this box to describe a disorganized person you know or a disorganized TV character.

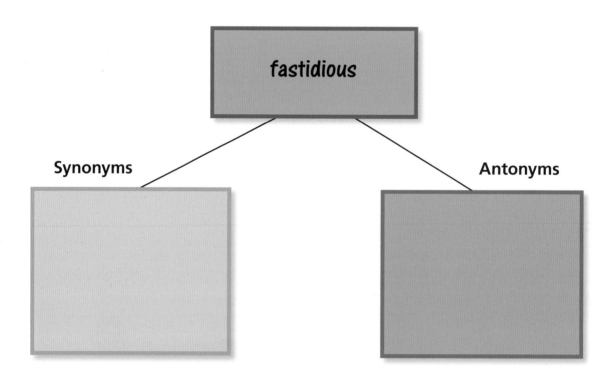

fastidious

Synonyms

Antonyms

Young People Who Made a Difference

Water, Anyone?

When 6-year-old Ryan Hreljac learned that people without access to clean water would become very sick or even die, he took action. He earned $70 by doing extra chores and donated the money toward building a well for people who inhabit Africa. Since this first well was dug in Uganda, Ryan has worked with several nonprofit agencies to build more wells. By the time he turned 15 in 2006, Ryan had helped raise more than $1.5 million to build 254 wells in 11 countries!

Ibrahim's Law

After his 16-month-old brother fell through a badly equipped fire escape and died, Abdul Hafiz set out to change state and federal laws even though he was only 8 years old. With the help of his second-grade teacher and classmates, Abdul led a movement to pass a bill known as "Ibrahim's Law." If passed, the law would apply to all New York City apartment buildings that housed children under the age of 10. These buildings would be required to have safety gates affixed to the fire escapes. By the time you read this, "Ibrahim's Law" may have passed.

A Hero to the Homeless

17-year-old Francesca Karle never thought she would achieve hero status when she made a short movie about homeless people. She was simply trying to earn a Girl Scout award. When *On the River's Edge* premiered, Francesca raised more than $25,000 for agencies that help homeless people. But raising money for the homeless isn't the real reason why Francesca has become a hero. Unlike many who maliciously scorn the problems of the homeless, Francesca helped restore their sense of dignity and self-respect.

> **"** *You must be the change you wish to see in the world.* **"**
> —Mohandas Gandhi

A Hero

A hero is you.
A hero is me.
To be a hero is my destiny.
In the face of danger, I'll be clever and sure footed.
I'll solve any problem, incipient or deep rooted
Fighting for peace with justice as my sword,
I'll stand for those who are mocked or ignored.
In my quest to show kindness, I'll work and I'll try.
I won't give up when things go awry.
When others are certain that all hope is lost,
I'll keep helping others regardless the cost.
A hero is you.
A hero is me.
To be a hero is my destiny.

Rev Up Your Writing

You've just read about real-life heroes—ordinary people who do extraordinary things for others. Write about a person you know or have heard about who did something to make another person's life better. Use as many of the vocabulary words as possible but make sense.

Can You Relate?

Copy this graphic organizer onto a separate piece of paper. Match the following words with their related vocabulary word. If a word relates to more than one vocabulary word, explain why.

abhor   If you abhor something, you hate it intensely.

beleaguer   If you beleaguer a person, you bother him or her continually.

collude   If you collude with someone, you work together to do something deceitful.

contemptuous   If you are contemptuous of something, you do not like or respect it at all.

debase   If you debase something, you make it seem less valuable.

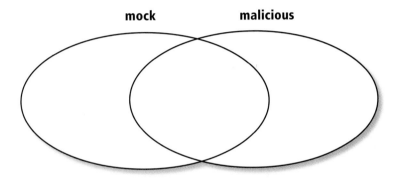

mock   malicious

In Your Own Words

Respond to one of the following prompts on a separate piece of paper. As you respond, use as many of the vocabulary words as possible. Be creative but make sense!

▶ Write about a time when you or someone you know had to wear a unique uniform or costume. What was the event? How did you feel about what you wore?

▶ Write a thank you letter to someone you admire because he or she works hard to help others.

▶ Write about a topic of your choice.

VOCABULARY

fastidious
awry
gingerly
malicious
mock
fabrication
inhabit
affix
incipient
mutate

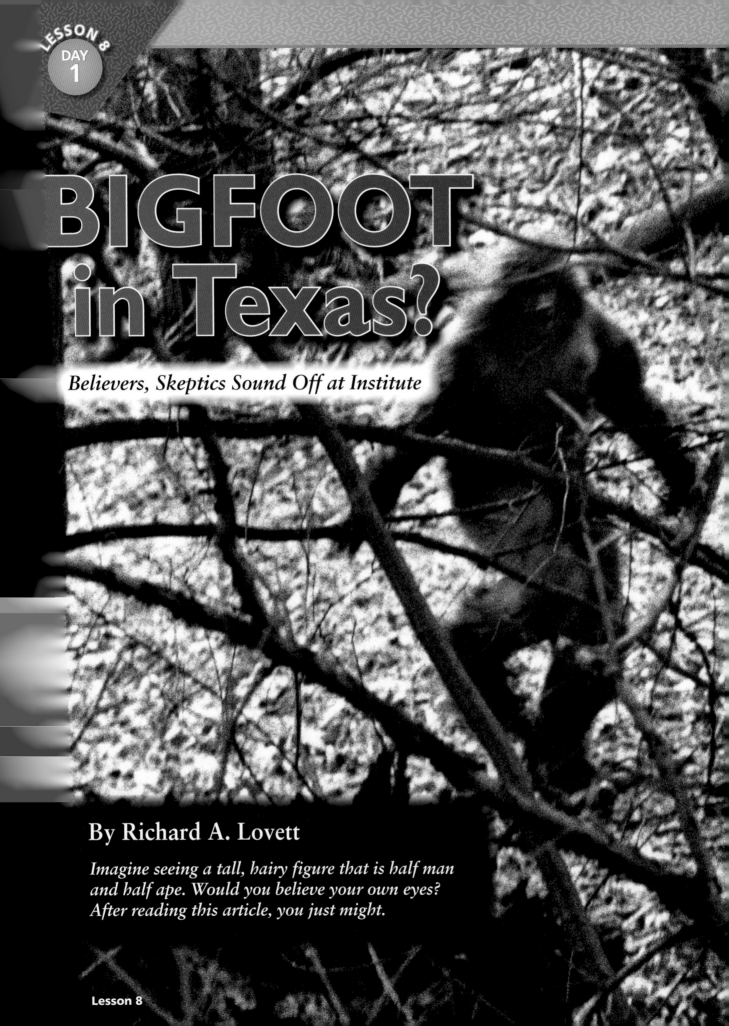

BIGFOOT in Texas?

Believers, Skeptics Sound Off at Institute

By Richard A. Lovett

Imagine seeing a tall, hairy figure that is half man and half ape. Would you believe your own eyes? After reading this article, you just might.

In 1994 Craig Woolheater and his wife were driving at night from New Orleans to Dallas, Texas. Somewhere in the swampy woods near Alexandria, Louisiana, he saw something at the side of the road. It was covered with hair, about seven feet tall, and walked on two legs.

"Did you see what I saw?" he asked his wife.

"Yes," she said, and they concluded that while they couldn't prove it, the most likely explanation was that they'd seen the creature once known to the Indians as the wild man or the lost giant.

In other words, he says, they'd seen Bigfoot, or the "Woolly Booger," as he's sometimes called in these parts.

"People think that Bigfoot is a Pacific Northwest phenomenon," said Woolheater, who is now director of the Texas Bigfoot Research Center outside of Dallas. "But there have been sightings in every state of the Union except Hawaii."

"Here in Texas," he added, "We have 22 million acres (9 million hectares) of forestland. In the four-state region [Texas, Oklahoma, Arkansas, and Louisiana] there are 65 million acres [26,000,000 hectares]. That's equivalent to the entire state of Oregon—not just the forest, but the entire state [much of Oregon is desert]."

"We have hundreds of eyewitness reports, footprint casts, hair samples—just as in the Pacific Northwest," Woolheater said.

Local Myths

Texas and neighboring states have a long history of sightings.

Local Native American lore[1] is replete with legends of giant, shaggy men. Sightings by white settlers date back to the "Wild Woman of the Navidad," a Bigfoot-like creature reportedly observed in 1837 along the Navidad River near the present-day town of Victoria, Texas.

Other 19th-century reports describe oversize, barefoot footprints and a creature covered in short, brown hair. The beast, it was said, moved quickly enough to elude efforts to lasso it from horseback.

Renewed attention came in 1969, Woolheater says, when sightings of the "Lake Worth Monster" were reported by hundreds of people, including police officers, practically on the fringes of metropolitan Fort Worth.

FOOTNOTES
[1] *lore:* traditional stories

"Throughout the seventies and eighties, there were a lot of newspaper articles telling of sightings in East Texas," Woolheater added.

Recently Woolheater helped organize "Bigfoot in Texas?"—a museum exhibition at the Institute of Texan Cultures at the University of Texas, San Antonio. The show opened April 7, and runs through July 30.

The Texas Bigfoot exhibition includes a recreation of an East Texas thicket, footprint casts, and a documentary called *Sasquatch:*[2] *Legend Meets Science*. During the accompanying lecture series, believers and skeptics alike are addressing such topics as folklore and field evidence.

The institute takes no position on whether the Lone Star[3] Sasquatch exists. But Woolheater and his colleagues managed to impress Willie Mendez, project director for the exhibit.

"I was really skeptical myself," Mendez said, until he met Woolheater's group.

They are "really credible people," Mendez added.

"Why would these people lie? They're not making any money off it, and they know they're going to get ridiculed. But they stand their ground."

"Poor Quality" Evidence

There is no credible evidence for the existence of Bigfoot, says Joe Nickell, senior research fellow for the Committee for the Scientific Investigation of Claims of the Paranormal, an Amherst, New York-based debunking organization that publishes a bimonthly magazine called *Skeptical Inquirer*.

"Or to put it another way," he said, "there's really quite a lot of evidence, but unfortunately it's very poor quality."

That's a problem for Bigfoot-believers, Nickell says, because if the creature really does exist, then it must exist in fairly substantial numbers. Otherwise, it would long ago have gone extinct.

"Not a single carcass has been found," he said.

"While we can't *prove* Bigfoot doesn't exist," he added, "it's fair to point out that we can't prove that the tooth fairy doesn't exist. We can't *prove* that there are no leprechauns."

The Bigfoot myth, Nickell suggests, is fueled by human hopes and fears. In that manner, he continues, it is similar to other myths.

"We are hopeful that we are not alone in the universe, so we believe in extraterrestrials," he said. "We are fearful of the unknown, so we imagine monsters and sinister aliens."

FOOTNOTES
[2] *Sasquatch:* another name for Bigfoot
[3] *Lone Star:* a reference to Texas (the Lone Star State)

"I think Bigfoot represents an artifact from a vanishing world. It's tempting to think that some early cousin of ours is still around. Extraterrestrials are futuristic versions of us. Bigfoot is our beastly cousin from the past."

Woolheater, of the Texas Bigfoot Research Center, agreed that there are "a whole lot of questions and not many answers."

"What we're trying to do," he said, "is get some answers and gather hard evidence."

"I think we're dealing with an animal that is fairly rare," Woolheater added.

"Estimates range from 2,000 to maybe 4,000 across the United States. So you're talking about something that is probably a hundred times more rare than a black bear, and certainly a lot more rare than a mountain lion, and those animals aren't seen all that often," Woolheater said.

"I think that, like most animals, when they're sick, dying, or injured, they go off to a secluded place—they don't just drop dead in the middle of the forest."

Meanwhile, the Institute of Texan Cultures is taking a democratic approach.

The final portion of the exhibition gives visitors a chance to vote on whether or not they believe the evidence is credible.

On the first day, Woolheater says, yeas outweighed nays 178 to 53.

Explain Yourself

Answer each question on a separate piece of paper. Be sure to explain your answers.

1. Would a baseball game be considered a **phenomenon**? Why or why not?

2. Would a backpack that is **replete** with pencils be easy to carry? Explain.

3. Which is more likely to **elude** capture, a cheetah or a turtle? Explain.

4. If you were **skeptical** about your uncle's cooking, would you eat his food? Explain.

5. Do you think newspapers are **credible** sources of information? Why or why not?

6. How could you **debunk** your friend's claim that he can beat you at arm wrestling? Explain.

7. If you had a **substantial** number of goldfish, what size tank would you need? Explain.

8. Is it hard to believe someone who says **implausible** things? Why or why not?

9. Would you be likely to make a **conjecture** about someone you just met? Why or why not?

10. Would you want to spend **fraudulent** money? Explain.

phenomenon   A phenomenon is a rare or unusually important event.

replete   Something that is replete is almost completely filled.

elude   If you elude something that is chasing you, you escape from it using cleverness and skill.

skeptical   If you are skeptical about something, you doubt that it's true.

credible   Someone or something that is credible can be trusted or believed.

debunk   If you debunk some idea or belief that people have, you show proof that it is not true or real.

substantial   When there is a substantial amount of something, there is a lot of it.

implausible   A story that is implausible is so unlikely that it's hard to believe.

conjecture   A conjecture is an opinion you form without much proof.

fraudulent   If someone's words or actions are fraudulent, they are meant to be false or dishonest.

Take It Further

Complete these sentences on a separate piece of paper.

1. The class knew they were seeing a **phenomenon** because . . .

2. The lake was **replete** with fish because . . .

3. To **elude** the dodgeballs, Sarah . . .

4. My dad was **skeptical** when I told him . . .

5. Andrew knew the Web site was **credible** because . . .

6. Anil **debunked** my theory about cafeteria food by . . .

7. Since I had **substantial** time to study for the test, I . . .

8. Yi's excuse was **implausible** because . . .

9. Aunt Amy's **conjecture** about rock singers was . . .

10. Muhammad proved the news article was **fraudulent** by . . .

Explore It

You know the word *implausible* by now, but are you familiar with two of its common antonyms, *probable* and *reasonable*?

probable
If something is probable, it is likely to be true or to happen.

reasonable
If something is reasonable, it is sensible and based on evidence.

> Working in a small group, make up three short stories. Make the events of one story implausible, the second probable, and the third reasonable. Remember that the outcome of each story will change depending on which word is used. Be prepared to share and explain your work!

One, Two, Three Peaks

What can you do in 24 hours?
You can fly from New York City to Sydney, Australia.
You can watch 24 shows on TV.
How about climbing three mountains?
By the way, they're in three different countries.

It sounds implausible, but people in Great Britain do it every year. It's called the Three Peaks Challenge, and people do it for charity or just for fun. To become a three-peak athlete, all you have to do is climb the tallest mountain in England, in Scotland, and in Wales; plus travel between the three, in 24 hours.

How do you pull it off? Luckily, the three mountains aren't that far apart. They're all on the island of Great Britain and the driving time from one mountain to the next is only 5 to 6 hours. The best time of year to climb is in June, when the days are longer.

Substantial team support, the order of the mountains, and timing are also critical. Most athletes tackle the mountains with a group for support and safety. They also have drivers who have the energy to zip from country to country safely. Their vehicles are replete with supplies, including food, water, and clothes.

Interested? Round up your gear, a pack of friends, and become an official three-peak athlete!

Ben Nevis in Scotland

Scafell Pike in Britain

Snowdon in Wales

K2

The world's second highest mountain is second to none. With storms and avalanches, Asia's K2 is a bigger challenge than Everest. Fewer people have climbed K2 than Everest, and more have died trying.

High Points
of the High Peaks

Climbing the Three Peaks of Great Britain is a challenge, but some mountains are taller and more dangerous than all three put together! Here are a few of the most dangerous mountains to climb in the world.

Kilimanjaro

Volcanoes are hot, right? Kilimanjaro's three peaks debunk that idea. They were once active volcanoes, but today the mountaintop is covered with the only glaciers in Africa.

Mount Jaya

It's a small world . . . and you can find it all on Oceania's Mt. Jaya! The mountain rises from tropical jungles to a snow-capped peak. On the way up, you can find a sampling of plants from many of the world's environments.

Mount Everest

Mt. Everest, located in Asia, is the tallest mountain on Earth. Although the summit eluded climbers for years, the mountain gets many visitors today. Its youngest climber was a 15-year-old girl.

Rev Up Your Writing

Mountain climbing can be an amazing and challenging experience. Write about a time when you or someone you know participated in a challenging physical activity. Use as many of the vocabulary words as possible but make sense.

Word Organizer

Copy this graphic organizer onto a separate piece of paper.

List things that a person does to prove him or herself to be credible and write your answers under the person column. Then list things that a person does to prove a piece of writing is credible and write your answers under the writing column. Explain your answers.

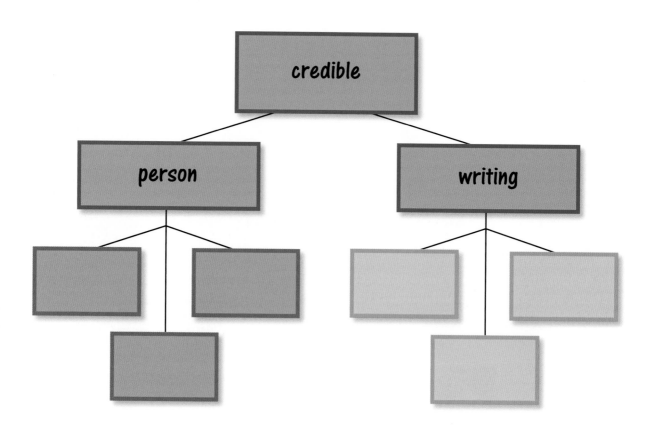

THE BIG AIR

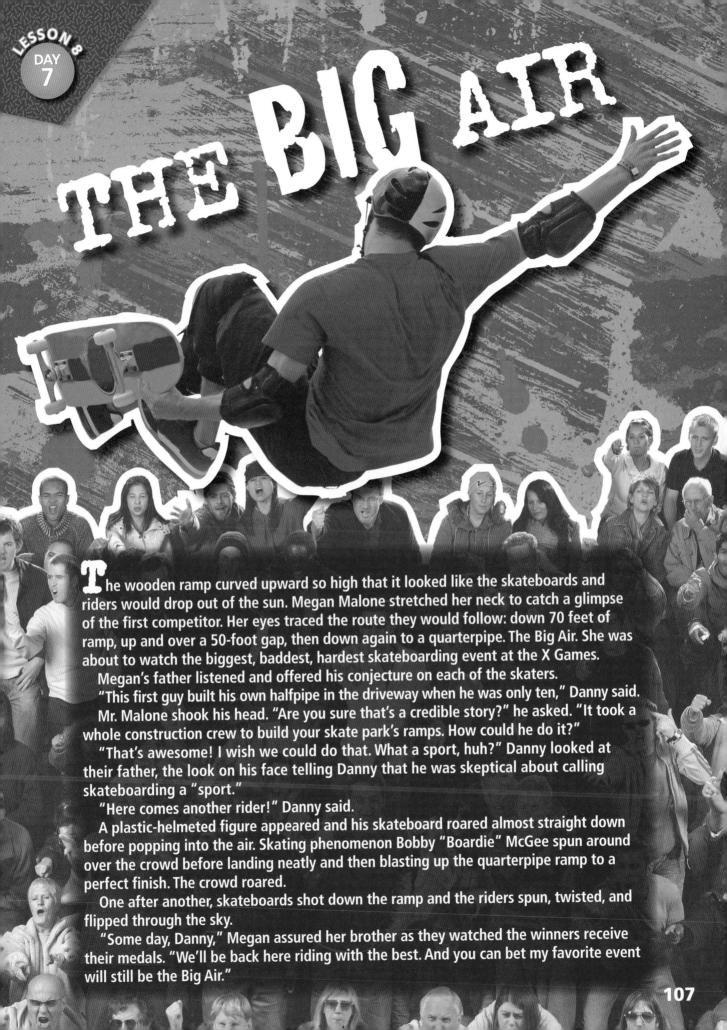

The wooden ramp curved upward so high that it looked like the skateboards and riders would drop out of the sun. Megan Malone stretched her neck to catch a glimpse of the first competitor. Her eyes traced the route they would follow: down 70 feet of ramp, up and over a 50-foot gap, then down again to a quarterpipe. The Big Air. She was about to watch the biggest, baddest, hardest skateboarding event at the X Games.

Megan's father listened and offered his conjecture on each of the skaters.

"This first guy built his own halfpipe in the driveway when he was only ten," Danny said.

Mr. Malone shook his head. "Are you sure that's a credible story?" he asked. "It took a whole construction crew to build your skate park's ramps. How could he do it?"

"That's awesome! I wish we could do that. What a sport, huh?" Danny looked at their father, the look on his face telling Danny that he was skeptical about calling skateboarding a "sport."

"Here comes another rider!" Danny said.

A plastic-helmeted figure appeared and his skateboard roared almost straight down before popping into the air. Skating phenomenon Bobby "Boardie" McGee spun around over the crowd before landing neatly and then blasting up the quarterpipe ramp to a perfect finish. The crowd roared.

One after another, skateboards shot down the ramp and the riders spun, twisted, and flipped through the sky.

"Some day, Danny," Megan assured her brother as they watched the winners receive their medals. "We'll be back here riding with the best. And you can bet my favorite event will still be the Big Air."

eXtreme POSTCARDS

Hey bros,

Cowabunga from Alaska, my friends! I told you surfing wasn't just for the tropics—the waves up here are totally sweet. Cold—but sweet. The salmon fishing is pretty good, too. This trip was worth the wetsuit!

Peace,
Eddy

Dear Nikos,

This photo is not fraudulent. After getting our skydiving license, Josh and I had a sky wedding. Check this out—the ceremony was held at 14,000 feet! Still haven't figured out who caught the bouquet. Will send more pictures soon.

—Carla

Nikos st.

427 Broa

Tacoma,

Rev Up Your Writing

You've just read about some incredible sports. What's the strangest sport or hobby you've ever heard of? Write a description of this hobby or sport. Use as many of the vocabulary words as possible but make sense.

Can You Relate?

Copy this graphic organizer onto a separate piece of paper. Match the following words with their related vocabulary word. If a word relates to more than one vocabulary word, explain why.

alleged   An alleged event is assumed to be true but not proven.
coherent   If an argument is coherent, it is very clear and sensible.
fallacious   If an idea is fallacious, it is wrong because it is based on incorrect information.
feasible   If something is feasible, it is capable of being done.
inconceivable   If a story is inconceivable, it is impossible to imagine or understand.

implausible	credible	conjecture

In Your Own Words

Respond to one of the following prompts on a separate piece of paper. As you respond, use as many of the vocabulary words as possible. Be creative but make sense!

▶ Write about an interesting activity that you or someone you know does. Explain how and why you do this activity.

▶ Write a letter to a friend describing your favorite athlete or another person who you believe has great talent.

▶ Write about a topic of your choice.

VOCABULARY

phenomenon
replete
elude
skeptical
credible
debunk
substantial
implausible
conjecture
fraudulent

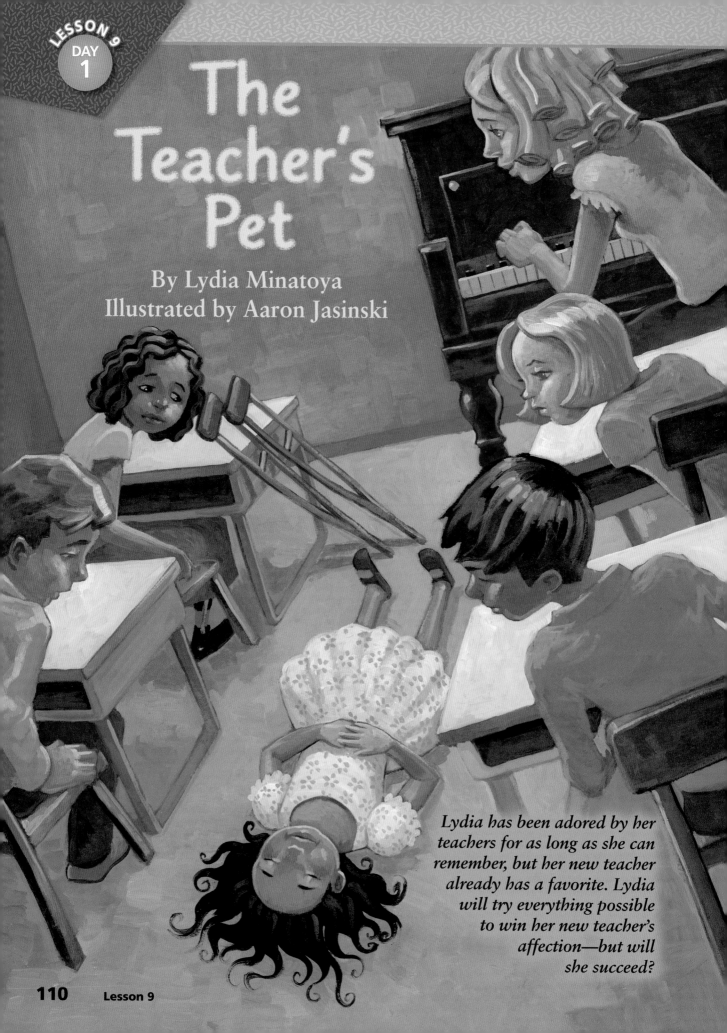

The Teacher's Pet

By Lydia Minatoya
Illustrated by Aaron Jasinski

Lydia has been adored by her teachers for as long as she can remember, but her new teacher already has a favorite. Lydia will try everything possible to win her new teacher's affection—but will she succeed?

When we lived in Albany, I always was the teacher's pet. "So tiny, so precocious,[1] so prettily dressed!" They thought I was a living doll and this was fine with me.

My father knew that the effusive praise would die. He had been through this with my sister. After five years of being a perfect darling, Misa had reached the age where students were tracked by ability. Then, the anger started. Misa had tested into the advanced track. It was impossible, the community declared. Misa was forbidden entry into advanced classes as long as there were white children being placed below her. In her defense, before an angry rabble,[2] my father made a presentation to the Board of Education.

But I was too young to know of this. I knew only that my teachers praised and petted me. They took me to other classes as an example. "Watch now, as Lydia demonstrates attentive behavior," they would croon as I was led to an empty desk at the head of the class. I had a routine. I would sit carefully, spreading my petticoated skirt neatly beneath me. I would pull my chair close to the desk, crossing my swinging legs at my snowy white anklets. I would fold my hands carefully on the desk before me and stare pensively[3] at the blackboard.

This routine won me few friends. The sixth-grade boys threw rocks at me. They danced around me in a tight circle, pulling at the corners of their eyes. "Ching Chong Chinaman," they chanted. But teachers loved me. When I was in first grade, a third-grade teacher went weeping to the principal. She begged to have me skipped. She was leaving to get married and wanted her turn with the dolly.

When we moved, the greatest shock was the knowledge that I had lost my charm. From the first, my teacher failed to notice me. But to me, it did not matter. I was in love. I watched her moods, her needs, her small vanities. I was determined to ingratiate.

FOOTNOTES
[1] *precocious:* having adult intelligence at an early age
[2] *rabble:* crowd
[3] *pensively:* thoughtfully

Miss Hempstead was a shimmering vision with a small upturned nose and eyes that were kewpie-doll[4] blue. Slender as a sylph,[5] she tripped around the classroom, all saucy in her high-heeled shoes. Whenever I looked at Miss Hempstead, I pitied the Albany teachers whom, formerly, I had adored. Poor old Miss Rosenberg. With a shiver of distaste, I recalled her loose fleshy arms, her mottled hands, the scent of lavender as she crushed me to her [chest].

Miss Hempstead had a pet of her own. Her name was Linda Sherlock. I watched Linda closely and plotted Miss Hempstead's courtship. The key was the piano. Miss Hempstead played the piano. She fancied herself a musical star. She sang songs from Broadway revues and shaped her students' reactions. "Getting to know you," she would sing. We would smile at her in a staged manner and position ourselves obediently at her feet.

Miss Hempstead was famous for her ability to soothe. Each day at rest time, she played the piano and sang soporific[6] songs. Linda Sherlock was the only child who succumbed. Routinely, Linda's head would bend and nod until she crumpled gracefully onto her folded arms. A tousled strand of blond hair would fall across her forehead. Miss Hempstead would end her song, would gently lower the keyboard cover. She would turn toward the restive eyes of the class. "Isn't she sweetness itself!" Miss Hempstead would declare. It made me want to vomit.

I was growing weary. My studiousness, my attentiveness, my fastidious grooming and pert poise: all were failing me. I changed my tactics. I became a problem. Miss Hempstead sent me home with nasty notes in sealed envelopes: Lydia is a slow child, a noisy child, her presence is disruptive. My mother looked at me with surprise, *"Nani desu ka?* Are you having problems with your teacher?" But I was tenacious. I pushed harder and harder, firmly caught in the obsessive need of the scorned.

One day I snapped.[7] As Miss Hempstead began to sing her wretched lullabies, my head dropped to the desk with a powerful CRACK! It lolled[8] there, briefly, then rolled toward the edge with a momentum that sent my entire body catapulting to the floor. Miss Hempstead's spine stretched slightly, like a cat that senses danger. Otherwise, she paid no heed. The linoleum floor was smooth and cool. It emitted a faint pleasant odor: a mixture of chalk dust and wax.

FOOTNOTES

[4] *kewpie-doll:* blue-eyed doll that was popular during the early 1900s

[5] *sylph:* imaginary flying spirit

[6] *soporific:* boring or tiresome

[7] *snapped:* lost control

[8] *lolled:* moved lazily

I began to snore heavily. The class sat electrified. There would be no drowsing today. The music went on and on. Finally, one boy could not stand it. "Miss Hempstead," he probed plaintively, "Lydia has fallen asleep on the floor!" Miss Hempstead did not turn. Her playing grew slightly strident but she did not falter.

I lay on the floor through rest time. I lay on the floor through math drill. I lay on the floor while my classmates scraped around me, pushing their sturdy little wooden desks into the configuration[9] for reading circle. It was not until penmanship practice that I finally stretched and stirred. I rose like Sleeping Beauty and slipped back to my seat. I smiled enigmatically.[10] A spell had been broken. I never again had a crush on a teacher.

FOOTNOTES

[9] *configuration:* arrangement
[10] *enigmatically:* in a mysterious way

Explain Yourself

Answer each question on a separate piece of paper. Be sure to explain your answers.

1. Is an **effusive** person likely to remain calm when meeting a rock star? Explain.

2. Would you expect people to **croon** in a library? Why or why not?

3. Would you **ingratiate** yourself to a substitute teacher? Why or why not?

4. Would it be **saucy** to tell a friend her new outfit looked terrible? Explain.

5. What might a person **succumb** to during a strict diet? Explain.

6. Would a runner trying to win a marathon have to be **tenacious**? Why or why not?

7. Are you likely to respond **plaintively** if you win a trip to your favorite amusement park? Why or why not?

8. If you were trying to take a nap, would you want to hear **strident** sounds? Explain.

9. Would you respond **flagrantly** to a neighbor who plays loud music all the time? Why or why not?

10. How might a **petulant** student respond to a request to write only in blue ink?

effusive   Effusive people show their feelings with a lot of enthusiasm.

croon   When you croon, you sing in a gentle and pleasant way.

ingratiate   When you ingratiate yourself to others, you do things to try to get them to like you.

saucy   Someone who is saucy is rude in a playful way.

succumb   If you succumb to something, you can't fight it anymore so you just give up.

tenacious   A tenacious person is very tough and doesn't give up easily.

plaintive   A plaintive sound or expression is sad and shows regret.

strident   A strident sound is harsh and unpleasant to listen to.

flagrant   A flagrant act is something very bad that is done without any attempt to hide it.

petulant   A petulant person is grouchy and often gets angry over things that aren't important.

Take It Further

Complete these sentences on a separate piece of paper.

1. After winning the contest, an **effusive** beauty pageant contestant . . .

2. When Lacy told the band she was a **crooner**, they . . .

3. If you wanted a job as a baby-sitter, you might **ingratiate** yourself to . . .

4. Jasmine's **saucy** personality caused other students to . . .

5. After a long, difficult game, Jackson finally **succumbed** when . . .

6. The new girl on the track team proved her **tenacity** when she . . .

7. After Roderick said goodbye to his girlfriend Kelly, he **plaintively** . . .

8. As usual, Melva gave a **strident** response by . . .

9. When his sister would not let him use the phone, Rashaad **flagrantly** . . .

10. Audrey left the dinner table looking **petulant** after . . .

LESSON 9
DAY 4

Explore It

You know the word *ingratiate* by now, but are you familiar with some colloquial terms that are similar to it? A colloquial term is a word or words that are used in everyday conversation but not normally used in writing. Some colloquial terms that have a similar meaning to *ingratiate* are *win someone's favor, get on someone's good side, yes-man,* or *bootlicker.*

Working with someone else, find colloquial terms for the vocabulary words *succumb* and *tenacious.*

A Rare Find!

Some animals are so rare that most people will never see them alive. Perhaps they are endangered. Perhaps they live in secluded areas. Some have even been banned! One thing's for sure, meeting one of these critters is an unusual experience.

The Great Bird Search

Looking for a way to earn some extra cash? Finding a bird's nest could earn you $10,000!

Don't get too effusive. The nest needs to belong to an ivory-billed woodpecker, a bird people used to think was extinct. Some researchers now think it might not have succumbed to extinction after all.

For the last 50 years, people have reported seeing ivory-billed woodpeckers and hearing the strident sounds of their pecking, but it wasn't until 2005 that anyone had a reliable sighting.

Now, a wildlife group is offering a $10,000 reward to anyone who can locate an ivory-billed woodpecker's home. If you're tenacious enough, you just might win the prize!

Can You Stomach This?

Look at the image of the frogs on this page. It looks like the larger frog is flagrantly eating the smaller one. Actually, the tiny frog is just coming out to play after spending about seven weeks in the mother frog's belly!

Unlike all other Australian frogs, gastric-brooding frogs develop inside the mother's belly. During this time, the mother does not eat anything. Once the young frogs are past tadpole stage, they hop off to explore their surroundings. These unique frogs started disappearing in the 1980s. The last gastric-brooding frog was seen in 1985.

Fish Out of Water

Whoever made up the phrase *like a fish out of water* obviously knew nothing about walking catfish. Using the fins on the front of its body as legs, this fish can actually walk out of water and across land.

These fish are not endangered, but are still hard to find. Because they jump from pond to pond, spreading diseases and eating other fish, some places have made them illegal to own. So if you catch one, throw it back before you get too emotionally attached!

Did you know:

- Walking catfish owners in Florida have lost fish because the fish literally walked away!
- In some parts of Florida, you may see walking catfish crossing the street, especially on rainy nights.

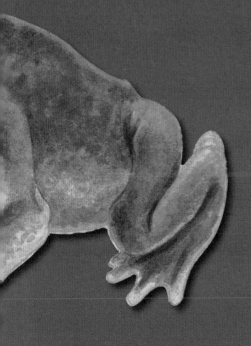

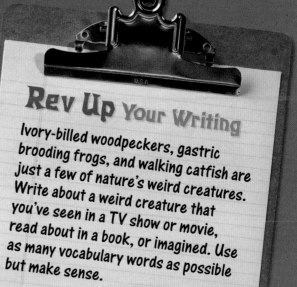

Rev Up Your Writing

Ivory-billed woodpeckers, gastric brooding frogs, and walking catfish are just a few of nature's weird creatures. Write about a weird creature that you've seen in a TV show or movie, read about in a book, or imagined. Use as many vocabulary words as possible but make sense.

Word Organizer

Copy this graphic organizer onto a separate piece of paper.

Think of words that describe the word *strident* and write your answers in the ovals. Then give examples of *strident* sounds and write your answers in the boxes. Explain your answers.

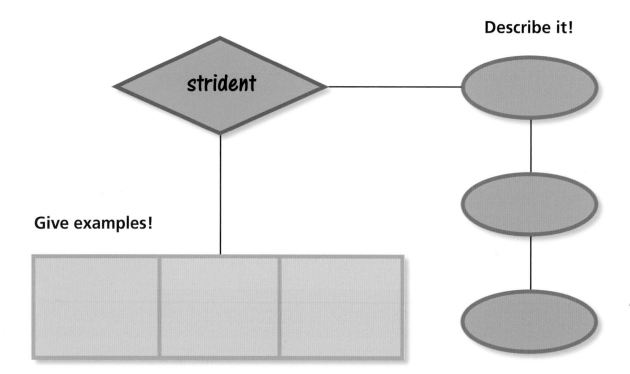

Describe it!

strident

Give examples!

REAL... or Really WEIRD?

There are many strange and mysterious animals in the world. Some are so rare and weird that most people don't believe they even exist. Some of the animals described below are 100% real and some have not been proven to exist. Try and guess which of the animals are which.

1 Puking Pickle

This creature is so effusive it barfs up its own guts whenever someone gets too close.

2 Dracula Dog

This saucy canine drains farm animals dry.

3 Reindeer Rabbit

A wild bunny that grows giant antlers.

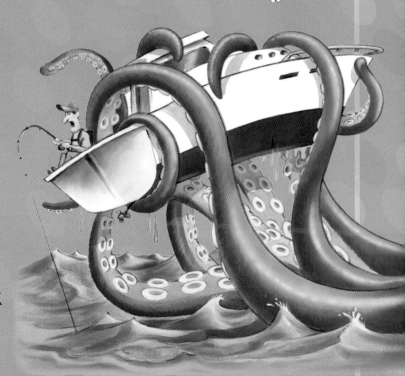

4 Massive Mollusk

This squishy giant fights with whales and sharks.

Go to the next page to see which are real . . .

1 The Sea Cucumber

When disturbed, these petulant creatures really do vomit their internal organs. But instead of killing the Sea Cucumber, the toxic organs scare away predators.

2 Chupacabra

Although many farmers in Latin America have plaintively claimed that a wild vampire dog killed and drained the blood of their livestock, no evidence has ever been found that this creature really exists.

3 The Jackalope

Most rabbits don't have a hard time ingratiating themselves to anyone, but jackalopes are said to strike fear in the people who see them. Even though no jackalope has ever been caught, the legendary creature is actually based on fact. A virus causes some jackrabbits to sprout growths from their heads that look a lot like horns.

4 The Giant Squid

For centuries, sailors have crooned songs about a mysterious giant squid that dragged ships down to the dark depths of the sea. But it hadn't been proven to exist until 2004, when a 20-foot-long Giant Squid was photographed alive. Humpback whales have been found with battle wounds from this car-sized monster's giant beak.

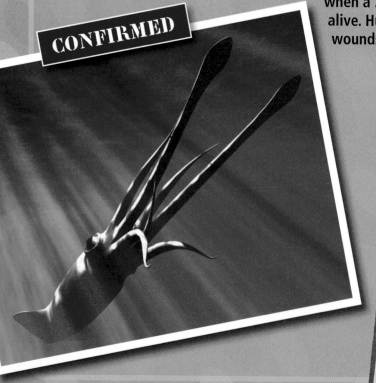

Rev Up Your Writing

You just read about animals that are so strange that some people doubt that they are real. Write about a time when you heard about something that was so strange you didn't believe it was true. Did it turn out to be true? Use as many vocabulary words as possible but make sense.

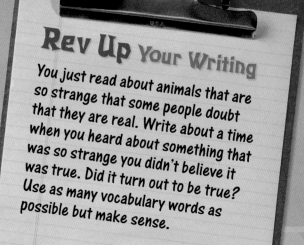

Can You Relate?

Copy this graphic organizer onto a separate piece of paper. Match the following words with their related vocabulary word. If a word relates to more than one vocabulary word, explain why.

impertinent   Someone who is impertinent is rude or disrespectful.
incorrigible   An incorrigible person will never change his or her bad habits.
jocular   If something is said or done in a jocular way, it is meant to be funny.
larceny   If someone is accused of larceny, he or she is accused of stealing.
obstreperous   Someone who is obstreperous is noisy and out of control.

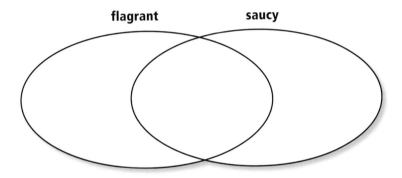

flagrant   saucy

In Your Own Words

Respond to one of the following prompts on a separate piece of paper. As you respond, use as many of the vocabulary words as possible. Be creative but make sense!

▶ Write about a time when you or someone you know took care of an animal or pet. What were the circumstances? Was the job difficult? Explain.

▶ Write a short poem that describes a mythical creature that you have read about or seen in a horror movie.

▶ Write about a topic of your choice.

VOCABULARY

effusive
croon
ingratiate
saucy
succumb
tenacious
plaintive
strident
flagrant
petulant

from
Long Walk to Freedom

By Nelson Mandela

In his autobiography, South African leader Nelson Mandela describes the difficulties he faced in his struggle for freedom and equality for all South Africans.

The policy of apartheid[1] created a deep and lasting wound in my country and my people. All of us will spend many years, if not generations, recovering from that profound hurt. But the decades of oppression and brutality had another, unintended effect, and that was that it produced the Oliver Tambos, the Walter Sisulus, the Chief Luthuäs, the Yusuf Dadoos, the Bram Fischers, the Robert Sobukwes of our time—men of such extraordinary courage, wisdom, and generosity that their like may never be known again. Perhaps it requires such depth of oppression to create such heights of character. My country is rich in the minerals and gems that lie beneath its soil, but I have always known that its greatest wealth is its people, finer and truer than the purest diamonds.

It is from these comrades in the struggle that I learned the meaning of courage. Time and again, I have seen men and women risk and give their lives for an idea. I have seen men stand up to attacks and torture without breaking, showing a strength and resiliency that defies the imagination. I learned that courage was not the absence of fear, but the triumph over it. I felt fear myself more times than I can remember, but I hid it behind a mask of boldness. The brave man is not he who does not feel afraid, but he who conquers that fear.

I never lost hope that this great transformation would occur. Not only because of the great heroes I have already cited, but because of the courage of the ordinary men and women of my country. I always knew that deep down in every human heart, there is mercy and generosity. No one is born hating another person because of the color of his skin, or his background, or his religion. People must learn to hate, and if they can learn to hate, they can be taught to love, for love comes more naturally to the human heart than its opposite. Even in the grimmest times in prison, when my comrades and I were pushed to our limits, I would see a glimmer of humanity in one of the guards, perhaps just for a second, but it was enough to reassure me and keep me going. Man's goodness is a flame that can be hidden but never extinguished.

FOOTNOTES

[1] *apartheid:* political system in South Africa that treated black South Africans unfairly

We took up the struggle with our eyes wide open, under no illusion[2] that the path would be an easy one. As a young man, when I joined the African National Congress,[3] I saw the price my comrades paid for their beliefs, and it was high. For myself, I have never regretted my commitment to the struggle, and I was always prepared to face the hardships that affected me personally. But my family paid a terrible price, perhaps too dear a price for my commitment.

In life, every man has twin obligations—obligations to his family, to his parents, to his wife and children; and he has an obligation to his people, his community, his country. In a civil and humane society, each man is able to fulfill those obligations according to his own inclinations and abilities. But in a country like South Africa, it was almost impossible for a man of my birth and color to fulfill both of those obligations. In South Africa, a man of color who attempted to live as a human being was punished and isolated. In South Africa, a man who tried to fulfill his duty to his people was inevitably ripped from his family and his home and was forced to live a life apart, a twilight existence of secrecy and rebellion. I did not in the beginning choose to place my people above my family, but in attempting to serve my people, I found that I was prevented from fulfilling my obligations as a son, a brother, a father, and a husband.

In that way, my commitment to my people, to the millions of South Africans I would never know or meet, was at the expense of the people I knew best and loved most. It was as simple and yet as incomprehensible as the moment a small child asks her father, "Why can you not be with us?" And the father must utter the terrible words: "There are other children like you, a great many of them . . ." and then one's voice trails off.

I was not born with a hunger to be free. I was born free—free in every way that I could know. Free to run in the fields near my mother's hut, free to swim in the clear stream that ran through my village, free to roast mealies[4] under the stars and ride the broad backs of slow-moving bulls. As long as I obeyed my father and abided by the customs of my tribe, I was not troubled by the laws of man or God.

FOOTNOTES
. . . .
[2] *illusion:* something that is not what it seems
[3] *African National Congress:* political group in South Africa that fought for civil rights and the end of apartheid
[4] *mealies:* corn cobs harvested before reaching maturity

It was only when I began to learn that my boyhood freedom was an illusion, when I discovered as a young man that my freedom had already been taken from me, that I began to hunger for it. At first, as a student, I wanted freedom only for myself, the transitory freedoms of being able to stay out at night, read what I pleased, and go where I chose. Later, as a young man in Johannesburg,[5] I yearned for the basic and honorable freedoms of achieving my potential, of earning my keep, of marrying and having a family—the freedom not to be obstructed in a lawful life.

But then I slowly saw that not only was I not free, but my brothers and sisters were not free. I saw that it was not just my freedom that was curtailed, but the freedom of everyone who looked like I did. That is when I joined the African National Congress, and that is when the hunger for my own freedom became the greater hunger for the freedom of my people. It was this desire for the freedom of my people to live their lives with dignity and self-respect that animated my life, that transformed a frightened young man into a bold one, that drove a law-abiding attorney to become a criminal, that turned a family-loving husband into a man without a home, that forced a life-loving man to live like a monk. I am no more virtuous or self-sacrificing than the next man, but I found that I could not even enjoy the poor and limited freedoms I was allowed when I knew my people were not free. Freedom is indivisible;[6] the chains on any one of my people were the chains on all of them, the chains on all of my people were the chains on me.

It was during those long and lonely years that my hunger for the freedom of my own people became a hunger for the freedom of all people, white and black. I knew as well as I knew anything that the oppressor must be liberated just as surely as the oppressed. A man who takes away another man's freedom is a prisoner of hatred, he is locked behind the bars of prejudice and narrow-mindedness.[7] I am not truly free if I am taking away someone else's freedom, just as surely as I am not free when my freedom is taken from me. The oppressed and the oppressor alike are robbed of their humanity.

FOOTNOTES

[5] *Johannesburg:* capital of South Africa

[6] *indivisible:* impossible to separate

[7] *narrow-mindedness:* the state of being unwilling or unable to see beyond one's own beliefs

When I walked out of prison, that was my mission, to liberate[8] the oppressed and the oppressor both. Some say that has now been achieved. But I know that that is not the case. The truth is that we are not yet free; we have merely achieved the freedom to be free, the right not to be oppressed. We have not taken the final step of our journey, but the first step on a longer and even more difficult road. For to be free is not merely to cast off one's chains, but to live in a way that respects and enhances[9] the freedom of others. The true test of our devotion to freedom is just beginning.

I have walked that long road to freedom. I have tried not to falter; I have made missteps[10] along the way. But I have discovered the secret that after climbing a great hill, one only finds that there are many more hills to climb. I have taken a moment here to rest, to steal a view of the glorious vista[11] that surrounds me, to look back on the distance I have come. But I can rest only for a moment, for with freedom come responsibilities, and I dare not linger, for my long walk is not yet ended.

FOOTNOTES
....
[8] *liberate:* set free
[9] *enhances:* makes better
[10] *missteps:* errors
[11] *vista:* a beautiful view

Explain Yourself

VOCABULARY

Answer each question on a separate piece of paper. Be sure to explain your answers.

1. How would a **resilient** person respond to getting cut from the basketball team? Explain.

2. If you had an **inclination** to play softball, what would you do? Explain.

3. If a confrontation with a bully was **inevitable**, what would you do? Why?

4. If someone said something **incomprehensible** to you, how would you respond? Why?

5. Would you want to **abide** by a decision you don't agree with? Explain.

6. Would you want **transitory** fame? Why or why not?

7. Would you want to **curtail** a bad habit? Explain.

8. What would a **virtuous** person do if he or she found another person's wallet on the ground? Explain.

9. Would an **altruistic** student ignore a classmate who is struggling to carry her books? Why or why not?

10. What **disparities** can you think of between your home and your school? Explain.

resilient   If you are resilient, you recover quickly from something bad that happened to you.

inclination   If you have an inclination about something, you have a feeling about it that helps you make a decision.

inevitable   If something is inevitable, it's going to happen no matter what.

incomprehensible   When someone or something is incomprehensible, it is impossible to understand.

abide   When you abide by a rule, you accept it and follow it.

transitory   If something is transitory, it only lasts for a moment.

curtail   When you curtail something, such as the amount of money you spend, you reduce it.

virtuous   Someone who is virtuous has high morals and always does the right thing.

altruistic   Altruistic people take care of other people's needs before they take care of their own.

disparity   If there is a disparity between two things, there is a difference between them.

Take It Further

Complete these sentences on a separate piece of paper.

1. My family showed how **resilient** we are when . . .

2. The artist had an **inclination** to . . .

3. We knew homework was **inevitable** because . . .

4. The directions for the game were **incomprehensible**, so . . .

5. The team **abided** by the rules because . . .

6. Alejandro knew the pain was **transitory**, so he . . .

7. Amy and Brett tried to **curtail** their hunger by . . .

8. Our **virtuous** grandmother told us to always . . .

9. Jen showed her **altruism** when she . . .

10. In her report, Marjorie wrote about the **disparity** between . . .

Explore It

How much do you know about where the words you use come from? For example, did you know that *curtail* originally referred to animal tails? The practice of shortening the tails of certain animals, such as dogs and horses, began long ago in Europe. The French word *courtault* and Latin word *curtus* contributed to the word *curtail* as a way of describing the act of shortening a tail. Today, the word refers to reducing the size or amount of something.

Think of three other words you use today that could have a history involving animals. Then, working with others, make up your own word histories! Explain the story behind each word: tell how it began, how it changed over the years, and what it means today. Be prepared to share your word histories with the class.

The Wrong Kind of Super . . . stitious!

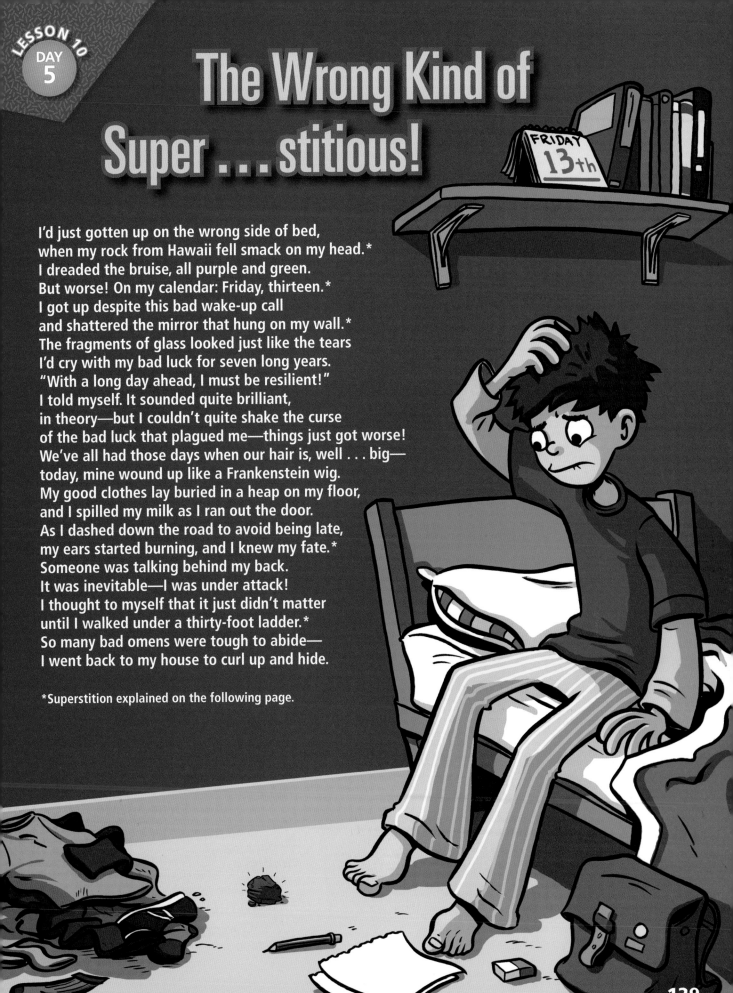

I'd just gotten up on the wrong side of bed,
when my rock from Hawaii fell smack on my head.*
I dreaded the bruise, all purple and green.
But worse! On my calendar: Friday, thirteen.*
I got up despite this bad wake-up call
and shattered the mirror that hung on my wall.*
The fragments of glass looked just like the tears
I'd cry with my bad luck for seven long years.
"With a long day ahead, I must be resilient!"
I told myself. It sounded quite brilliant,
in theory—but I couldn't quite shake the curse
of the bad luck that plagued me—things just got worse!
We've all had those days when our hair is, well . . . big—
today, mine wound up like a Frankenstein wig.
My good clothes lay buried in a heap on my floor,
and I spilled my milk as I ran out the door.
As I dashed down the road to avoid being late,
my ears started burning, and I knew my fate.*
Someone was talking behind my back.
It was inevitable—I was under attack!
I thought to myself that it just didn't matter
until I walked under a thirty-foot ladder.*
So many bad omens were tough to abide—
I went back to my house to curl up and hide.

*Superstition explained on the following page.

129

Superstitions Exposed!

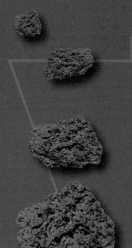

Rock from Hawaii

Legend has it that Pele, an ancient Hawaiian volcano goddess, regards all natural objects in Hawaii as her children. Tourists who take rocks as souvenirs are said to suffer terrible luck. Countless rocks are mailed back to Hawaii each year with the senders' pleas for forgiveness.

Burning Ears

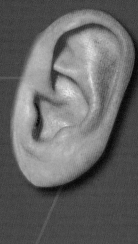

This superstition, dating back to Roman times, says that if your ears feel like they are burning, someone is talking about you. That superstition went on to suggest that if the sensation occurred in the right ear, the talk was good, but if it came from the left ear, it was bad.

Friday the 13th

In western culture, fear of Fridays and of the number "13" combine to form one unlucky day! Some historians trace the superstitions to early Christianity, while others look to ancient Norse culture. Despite the disparity, most people don't know why they are supposed to be afraid—they are simply taught to look out for bad luck on that dreaded Friday!

Walking under a Ladder

What could be so unlucky about walking under a ladder? One idea is that in medieval times, a leaning ladder resembled a gallows, a wooden frame where people were hanged. People who walked under a ladder were said to be doomed to die by hanging!

Breaking a Mirror

Looking into a mirror may give you more than a transitory glimpse of yourself; some say the human reflection is linked to the soul. Destroying a reflection (as in a mirror) is said to damage the soul and bring bad luck to that person. The "seven years" may be linked to an old belief that a person's life runs in seven-year cycles.

Rev Up Your Writing

You've just read about superstitions. Do you have any superstitions of your own? Write a short article explaining a superstition that you have or have heard about. Use as many of the vocabulary words as possible but make sense.

Word Organizer

Copy this graphic organizer onto a separate piece of paper.

List words that have almost the same meaning as *transitory* and write your answers in the web. Then tell about an event in your life that was transitory.

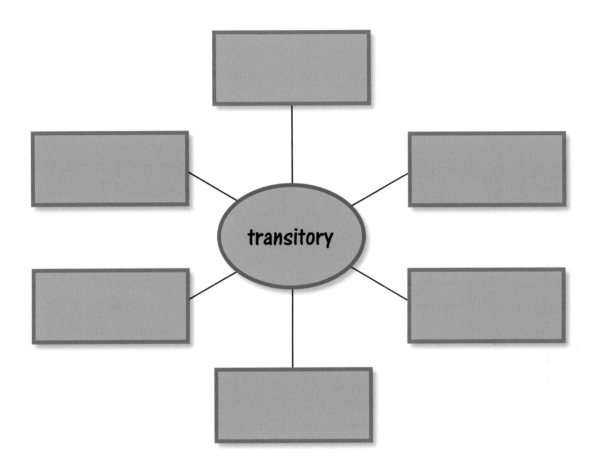

X-treme challenge

Have you ever had the inclination to run across the Sahara Desert carrying everything you'll need to survive on your back? To some, this may seem incomprehensible, but to the men and women who compete in the Four Deserts challenge, it's the experience of a lifetime.

**Four continents;
600 miles on foot;
the hottest, coldest, driest,
and windiest spots on Earth.**

What Is It?

The Four Deserts challenge is a series of multi-stage events that take place in the world's four largest deserts: the Gobi (the largest cold winter desert), the Atacama (the largest cool coastal desert), the Sahara (the largest subtropical desert), and Antarctica (the largest polar desert).

Each event is broken into six stages that take place over seven days. Participants must cover from 10 to 50 miles per day, for a total of 150 miles per event. If you complete all four events, you will have traveled by foot over 600 miles of the world's most unfriendly terrain.

You wouldn't be alone though. Teams of staff members and altruistic volunteers manage checkpoints every seven to eight miles along each route and supply competitors with water and any necessary medical attention. However, anything else you might need—food, bedding, clothing—you'll have to carry with you, so you might want to curtail the number of supplies that you bring!

The Gobi March™

LOCATION: China
CLIMATE: Temperatures can range from more than 100 degrees Fahrenheit during the day to below freezing at night, and there are occasional violent sandstorms.
TERRAIN: mostly rocky, but with occasional sand dunes up to 1,000 feet high

The Atacama Crossing™

LOCATION: Chile
CLIMATE: The Atacama Desert is the driest place on Earth—50 times drier than California's Death Valley; temperatures can range from 100 degrees Fahrenheit during the day to below freezing at night.
TERRAIN: river valleys, massive salt flats, and volcanoes

The Sahara Race™

LOCATION: Egypt
CLIMATE: The Sahara is the largest and hottest desert in the world. Daytime air temperatures can reach over 130 degrees Fahrenheit, and soil temperatures can reach over 170 degrees Fahrenheit.
TERRAIN: rocky mountains that give way to massive sand dunes and the occasional palm-filled oasis

The Last Desert™

LOCATION: Antarctica
CLIMATE: Average temperatures in Antarctica range from 41 degrees Fahrenheit to minus 31 degrees Fahrenheit in the summer months. Antarctica has the strongest winds on Earth, which can reach speeds of nearly 200 miles per hour.
TERRAIN: snow, ice, rocks, mud, and glacial-melt rivers

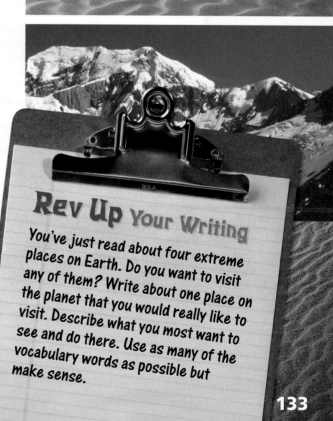

Sound like fun? It will take more than virtue to get you through the Four Deserts—it will take perseverance and an amazing tolerance for extremes!

Rev Up Your Writing

You've just read about four extreme places on Earth. Do you want to visit any of them? Write about one place on the planet that you would really like to visit. Describe what you most want to see and do there. Use as many of the vocabulary words as possible but make sense.

Can You Relate?

Copy this graphic organizer onto a separate piece of paper. Match the following words with their related vocabulary word. If a word relates to more than one vocabulary word, explain why.

empathetic   An empathetic person tries to imagine how other people feel.
knotty   A knotty question is extremely difficult to answer.
munificent   If you are munificent, you are very generous to others.
penchant   When you have a penchant for something, you really like it.
whim   A person with a whim changes his or her mind suddenly and unpredictably.

altruistic	incomprehensible	inclination

In Your Own Words

Respond to one of the following prompts on a separate piece of paper. As you respond, use as many of the vocabulary words as possible. Be creative but make sense!

▶ Write about a type of food from another culture that you enjoy. Describe the dish and explain why you like it.

▶ Do you think superstitions are true or just silly beliefs? Write a letter to your school paper arguing one way or the other. Try to convince the other students to agree with you!

▶ Write about a topic of your choice.

VOCABULARY

resilient
inclination
inevitable
incomprehensible
abide
transitory
curtail
virtuous
altruistic
disparity

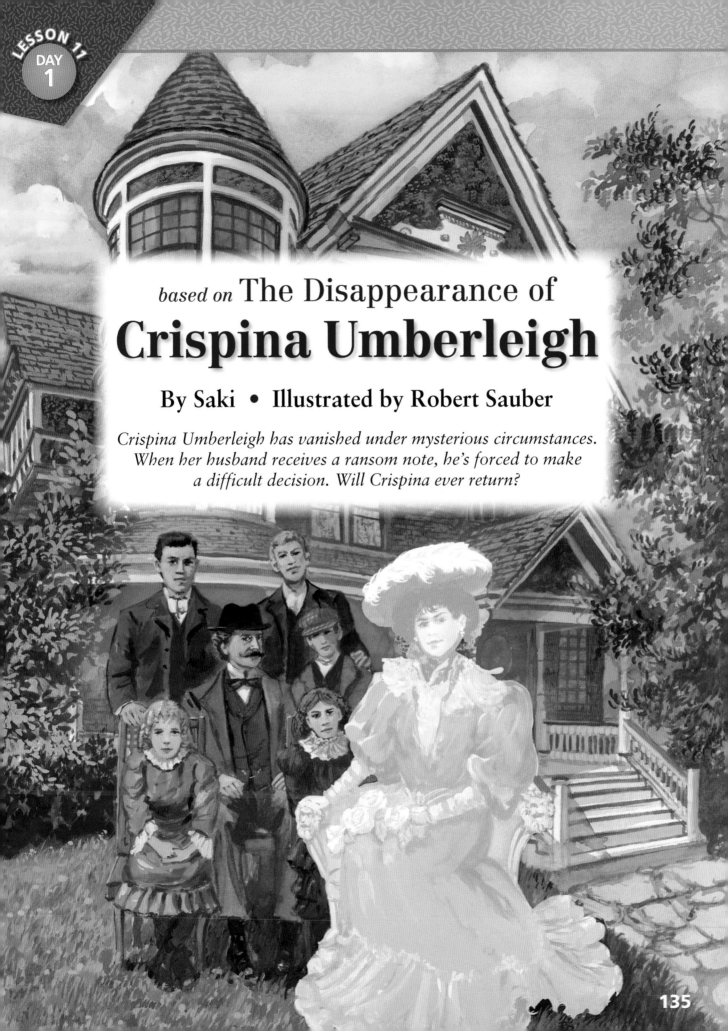

based on The Disappearance of

Crispina Umberleigh

By Saki • Illustrated by Robert Sauber

Crispina Umberleigh has vanished under mysterious circumstances.
When her husband receives a ransom note, he's forced to make
a difficult decision. Will Crispina ever return?

The family didn't exactly consider Mrs. Umberleigh's disappearance to be cause for bereavement. My uncle, Edward Umberleigh, was not by any means a weak individual—in fact in the world of politics he was considered a strong man—but there was no doubt that Crispina controlled him. Indeed I've never met any human being who was not frozen into subjection when brought into contact with her. Some people are born to command; Crispina Umberleigh was born to legislate, administrate, censor, license, ban, execute, and sit in judgment generally. If she was not born with that destiny she adopted it at an early age. Every one in the household came under her despotic sway and stayed there with complete submissiveness. As a nephew, I visited occasionally and thought of her merely as an epidemic,[1] disagreeable while it lasted but without any permanent effect. But her own sons and daughters stood in extreme fear of her; their studies, friendships, diet, amusements, and way of doing their hair were all controlled by the lady's will and pleasure. This will help you to understand the family's confusion when she suddenly and inexplicably vanished.

Of course the matter was put in the hands of the police, but it was kept out of the papers, and the generally accepted explanation of her withdrawal from society was that she had gone into a nursing home.

Bicycle riding had become quite popular among young women, but Crispina had refused to let her girls participate in the bicycle craze. So, upon her disappearance, the girls immediately bought themselves bicycles. The youngest boy let himself go to such an extent during his next semester that it had to be his last as far as that particular school was concerned. The elder boys developed a theory that their mother was wandering somewhere abroad and searched for her assiduously, mainly in a resort area where it was extremely unlikely that she would be found.

One day, my uncle got a message telling him that his wife had been kidnapped and smuggled out of the country; she was said to be hidden away in one of the islands off the coast of Norway in comfortable surroundings and well cared for. With the information came a demand for money; a lump sum of 2,000 pounds[2] was to be paid yearly. If he failed to pay this, she would be immediately returned to her family.

FOOTNOTES
. . . .
[1] *epidemic:* an outbreak of disease that attacks many people
[2] *pounds:* British money

It was certainly an inverted form of ransom, but if you had known my aunt, you would have wondered why the kidnappers hadn't put the figure higher.

When considering the ransom, my uncle had to think of others as well as himself. For the family to be forced to submit again to Crispina's control after having tasted the delights of freedom would have been a tragedy, and there were even wider considerations to be taken into account. He had gained a bolder and more powerful role in public affairs. From being merely a strong man in the political world, he began to be spoken of as the strong man. All this he knew would be jeopardized[3] if he once more dropped into the social position of simply Mrs. Umberleigh's husband. He was a rich man, and the 2,000 pounds a year, though not exactly a fleabite, did not seem an extravagant[4] price to pay to keep Crispina away. So he paid the yearly fees as punctually as one pays fire insurance. After each payment, an acknowledgment of the money arrived with a brief statement that Crispina was in good health and cheerful spirits.

The police came to my uncle from time to time to report on clues they had found, but I think they had their suspicions that he had more information than he had revealed. And then, after a disappearance of more than eight years, Crispina suddenly returned to the home she had left so mysteriously.

It turns out that she had never been captured. Her wandering away had been caused by a sudden and complete loss of memory. She usually dressed in the style of a high-class maid, and so she believed that she was one. She had wandered as far away as Birmingham[5] and found steady employment there. She had impressive energy and enthusiasm in putting people's rooms in order. It was only after being spoken to patronizingly that her memory was suddenly restored. "I think you forget who you are speaking to," she responded severely, even though she had only just remembered it herself.

All this time those who had required the ransom money had captured a purely make-believe prisoner. Someone who knew the family, probably a servant, bluffed a great deal of money out of Edward Umberleigh before the missing woman turned up.

FOOTNOTES
[3] *jeopardized:* put in danger
[4] *extravagant:* unreasonably high
[5] *Birmingham:* a city in England

Crispina discovered that her power over her children had been weakened by her absence. Her husband, however, never accomplished anything great in the political world after her return; he spent most of his time trying to explain to her the missing 16,000 pounds spread over eight years.

Explain Yourself

Answer each question on a separate piece of paper. Be sure to explain your answers.

1. Is a person experiencing **bereavement** likely to attend a party? Why or why not?

2. Would you want to live under the **subjection** of someone else? Why or why not?

3. Which is more likely to be **censored**, a popular music CD or a science textbook? Explain.

4. What would probably happen to a **despotic** class president? Explain.

5. Would you want a guard dog to be **submissive**? Explain.

6. If you worked **assiduously** on a school play, should you expect good reviews? Why or why not?

7. If you were driving a car, would you want to be **inverted** in the seat? Explain.

8. How would you react if your lab partner treated you **patronizingly**? Explain.

9. Who would you expect to say **caustic** things, a bully or a friend? Why?

10. When would it be appropriate to use **artifice**? Explain.

bereavement   Bereavement is the feeling of pain and loss you experience when a close friend or family member dies.

subjection   When people are forced into subjection, they are brought under complete control.

censor   Someone who censors something removes any part of it that is thought to be harmful or dangerous.

despotic   A despotic person uses his or her powers over others in an unfair and often cruel way.

submissive   Submissive people quietly do what others tell them to do.

assiduously   When you do something assiduously, you put a lot of effort and hard work into it.

inverted   Something that is inverted is upside down or opposite from what it usually is.

patronizingly   People who act patronizingly toward you treat you like they are smarter or better than you are.

caustic   Someone or something that is caustic is so harsh that it damages whatever it comes into contact with.

artifice   Artifice is the skillful and clever use of tricks, such as disguises, to fool others.

Take It Further

Complete these sentences on a separate piece of paper.

1. Jamal visited the **bereaved** family after . . .

2. After years of living in **subjection** to his older sister, Anthony finally . . .

3. When Ling speaks to her grandmother, she knows what she has to **censor** because . . .

4. Billy agreed that the **despotic** leader of their club should . . .

5. We trained the new puppy to be **submissive** by . . .

6. Before her first guitar performance, Helena **assiduously** . . .

7. The snowboarder was **inverted** when she . . .

8. When Brandi saw my test score, she **patronizingly** . . .

9. Bleach is **caustic**, so . . .

10. With a good deal of **artifice**, Cesar's friends . . .

Explore It

The word *censor*, "to remove any part of something thought to be harmful or dangerous," is often confused with the word *censure*, which means "to tell someone you strongly disagree with what they've done." There are other word pairs that are often confused for each other and used incorrectly. Here are a few examples:

accept = to receive   **except** = to leave out

affect = to influence   **effect** = the result

ensure = to make certain   **insure** = to protect

Work with a partner or in a group to write song lyrics using the word pairs listed above. If you can come up with any other word pairs like the ones above, use them as well. Be creative and prepare to share your song with the rest of the class.

Blind Video Gamer
Wows Competition

Brice Mellen enjoys subjecting his peers to his amazing skill at video games. That's not unusual for the average 17-year-old, but for Mellen, it's an amazing feat.

Mellen was born without sight because of Leber's disease, a rare disorder that causes damage to optic nerves. As a child, Mellen relied on his other senses to develop his video game skills.

That process wasn't always easy for Mellen, who began playing at age seven. It took years of assiduous practice for his skills to reach the level they are at today. He had to memorize joystick patterns and audio cues in order to play the games. Today, Mellen's so good at gaming that he's able to play with his back to the screen!

Mellen's hard work has paid off. These days, he can often be found at a local gaming center in Lincoln, Nebraska, controller in hand, crushing the competition. Some people think they can beat Mellen easily because of his disability, but Mellen doesn't let that bother him. In fact, he is more likely to welcome the challenge. He has inverted people's perceptions of what a person without sight is capable of. You won't find him patronizing any of the losers, however. Mellen admits that, although he is very good, he can be beat!

What's Your Gaming Style?

Take this quiz to find out.

1 The perfect video game must have—

A. great graphics.

B. an interesting story.

C. a multi-player option.

3 Video game violence—

A. should not be censored.

B. should be censored somewhat.

C. doesn't affect me one way or the other.

2 My ideal video game involves—

A. action heroes in exciting battles.

B. magical journeys to strange lands.

C. crazy sports competitions.

4 When I'm not playing video games, I'm usually—

A. watching an action-packed movie.

B. reading a good book.

C. playing sports.

If you chose...

Mostly As

You're an action gamer! As long as your game has awesome graphics and thrilling battles, you're happy.

Mostly Bs

You're an adventure gamer! You love games with long, complicated plots, things to discover, and mysteries to uncover.

Mostly Cs

You're a sports gamer! Any game starring your favorite athlete is perfect for you.

Rev Up Your Writing

Everyone has a favorite game. What type of games do you like? Write a plan for a game that you would like to design. Describe the graphics and action. Why would people want to play your game? Use as many of the vocabulary words as possible but make sense.

Word Organizer

Copy this graphic organizer onto a separate piece of paper.

List things that must be done assiduously in the top half of the Word Wheel.
List things that do not need to be done assiduously in the bottom half.

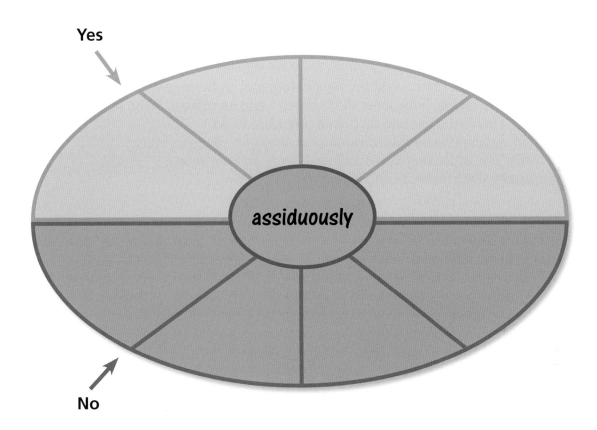

Yes

assiduously

No

What's in a Game?

Our eyes were glazed as we sat and played, my best friend Alice and I.
My new gaming system was the best that money could buy.
First we were soldiers saving the earth from despotic alien attack,
then we were quarterbacks, handing the football off to the running back.
Sometimes we would race our digital rides down virtual roads,
that is, until yesterday when we watched the video box explode.

"Your processor is fried!" said the repair store guy, as his glasses slid down his nose.
Bereaved, we asked, "How long 'til it's fixed?" and he replied, "Who knows?"
Alice and I hurried home and discussed just what to do.
We tried watching reality show reruns, but they only made us blue.
My father saw us looking bored and said, "Hey, come with me.
I have some things you can do for fun that don't involve TV!"

"Yeah, right," I shot back caustically. I wasn't too excited
when Dad led us to the attic. *He* was obviously delighted.
We pulled out some old boxes, but there were no discs to be seen!
Then Dad said, "These games kept me happy before video screens."
As Alice and I took our places submissively on the rug,
my father showed off his old board games, and I could only shrug.

Turns out this was not some artifice to make our lives more dull,
it was my father's way of easing up our painful video lull.
There were checkers and chess in there, of course, and games with battleships.
None had killer graphics, though some made squeaks and blips.
I had heard about Go Fish, but had never actually played it.
And had no idea there was a board game on surgery—until Dad displayed it.

In a day, the store clerk called my house; our system was done in a flash.
But Alice and I were playing trivia games and dealing in phony cash.
The video games still bring me joy at times, I really must admit.
But now I've discovered, to my dad's delight, it's the board games I can't quit.
So I ask you now, just what's in a game? Is it a 3-D graphic machine?
Or is there a game without video, a world without a screen?

Rev Up Your Writing

Discovering new things can be exciting! What activity do you enjoy that you would recommend to others? Why would you recommend it? Write a letter to a friend persuading him or her to take up your activity. Use as many vocabulary words as possible but make sense.

Can You Relate?

Copy this graphic organizer onto a separate piece of paper. Match the following words with their related vocabulary word. If a word relates to more than one vocabulary word, explain why.

concede   If you concede something, you unwillingly give people what they want.

imperious   Imperious people act proud and bossy.

injunction   An injunction is a command or an order to stop doing something.

malevolent   If people are malevolent, they want to harm others on purpose.

sycophant   A sycophant is someone who tries to please others in order to get what he or she wants.

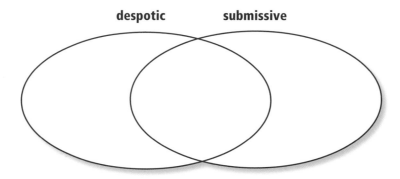

despotic   submissive

In Your Own Words

Respond to one of the following prompts on a separate piece of paper. As you respond, use as many of the vocabulary words as possible. Be creative but make sense!

▶ Write about a time when you or a friend participated in a competition. What did the competitors have to do? Who won? What did you learn by participating in the competition?

▶ Write a biography about someone you respect. Explain the qualities you admire about this person, and tell why he or she is worthy of praise.

▶ Write about a topic of your choice.

VOCABULARY

bereavement
subjection
censor
despotic
submissive
assiduously
inverted
patronizingly
caustic
artifice

from

THE LETTER "A"

By Christy Brown

Can a left foot perform a miracle? As Christy Brown struggles with a medical condition that makes communication nearly impossible, he realizes that the answer to this question could change his life forever.

It happened so quickly, so simply after all the years of waiting and uncertainty, that I can see and feel the whole scene as if it had happened last week. It was the afternoon of a cold, gray December day. The streets outside glistened with snow, the white sparkling flakes stuck and melted on the windowpanes and hung on the boughs of the trees like molten silver. The wind howled dismally, whipping up little whirling columns of snow that rose and fell at every fresh gust. And over all, the dull, murky sky stretched like a dark canopy, a vast infinity of grayness.

Inside, all the family were gathered round the big kitchen fire that lit up the little room with a warm glow and made giant shadows dance on the walls and ceiling.

In a corner Mona and Paddy were sitting, huddled together, a few torn school primers[1] before them. They were writing down little sums onto an old chipped slate, using a bright piece of yellow chalk. I was close to them, propped up by a few pillows against the wall, watching.

It was the chalk that attracted me so much. It was a long, slender stick of vivid yellow. I had never seen anything like it before, and it showed up so well against the black surface of the slate that I was fascinated by it as much as if it had been a stick of gold.

Suddenly, I wanted desperately to do what my sister was doing. Then—without thinking or knowing exactly what I was doing, I reached out and took the stick of chalk out of my sister's hand—with my left foot.

I do not know why I used my left foot to do this. It is a puzzle to many people as well as to myself, for, although I had displayed a curious interest in my toes at an early age, I had never attempted before this to use either of my feet in any way. They could have been as useless to me as were my hands. That day, however, my left foot, apparently by its own volition, reached out and very impolitely took the chalk out of my sister's hand.

FOOTNOTES
[1] *school primers:* schoolbooks

I held it tightly between my toes, and, acting on an impulse, made a wild sort of scribble with it on the slate. Next moment I stopped, a bit dazed, surprised, looking down at the stick of yellow chalk stuck between my toes, not knowing what to do with it next, hardly knowing how it got there. Then I looked up and became aware that everyone had stopped talking and was staring at me silently. Nobody stirred. Mona, her black curls framing her chubby little face, stared at me with great big eyes and open mouth. Across the open hearth, his face lit by flames, sat my father, leaning forward, hands outspread on his knees, his shoulders tense. I felt the sweat break out on my forehead.

My mother came in from the pantry with a steaming pot in her hand. She stopped midway between the table and the fire, feeling the tension flowing through the room. She followed their stare and saw me in the corner. Her eyes looked from my face down to my foot, with the chalk gripped between my toes. She put down the pot.

Then she crossed over to me and knelt down beside me, as she had done so many times before.

"I'll show you what to do with it, Chris," she said, very slowly and in a queer, choked way, her face flushed as if with some inner excitement.

Taking another piece of chalk from Mona, she hesitated, then very deliberately drew, on the floor in front of me, *the single letter "A."*

"Copy that," she said, looking steadily at me. "Copy it, Christy."

I couldn't.

I looked about me, looked around at the faces that were turned towards me, tense, excited faces that were at that moment frozen, immobile, eager, waiting for a miracle in their midst.

The stillness was profound. The room was full of flame and shadow that danced before my eyes and lulled my taut nerves into a sort of waking sleep. I could hear the sound of the water tap dripping in the pantry, the loud ticking of the clock on the mantel shelf, and the soft hiss and crackle of the logs on the open hearth.

I tried again. I put out my foot and made a wild jerking stab with the chalk which produced a very crooked line and nothing more. Mother held the slate steady for me.

"Try again, Chris," she whispered in my ear. "Again."

I did. I stiffened my body and put my left foot out again, for the third time. I drew one side of the letter. I drew half the other side. Then the stick of chalk broke and I was left with a stump. I wanted to fling it away and give up. Then I felt my mother's hand on my shoulder. I tried once more. Out went my foot. I shook, I sweated and strained every muscle. My hands were so tightly clenched that my fingernails bit into the flesh. I set my teeth so hard that I nearly pierced my lower lip. Everything in the room swam[2] till the faces around me were mere patches of white. But—I drew it—*the letter "A."* There it was on the floor before me. Shaky, with awkward, wobbly sides and a very uneven center line. But it *was* the letter "A." I looked up. I saw my mother's face for a moment, tears on her cheeks. Then my father stooped and hoisted me onto his shoulder.

I had done it! I had started—the thing that was to give my mind its chance of expressing itself. True, I couldn't speak with my lips. But now I would speak through something more lasting than spoken words—written words.

That one letter, scrawled on the floor with a broken bit of yellow chalk gripped between my toes, was my road to a new world, my key to mental freedom. It was to provide a source of relaxation to the tense, taut thing that was I, which panted for expression behind a twisted mouth.

Explain Yourself

Answer each question on a separate piece of paper. Be sure to explain your answers.

1. Would you want the change in your pocket to become **molten**? Explain.

2. What might make a mirror appear **murky**? Why?

3. When would it be beneficial not to act on your own **volition**? Explain.

4. What would likely cause a person to become **flushed**? Why?

5. Would you want to own an **immobile** sports car? Why or why not?

6. When would you want to give a **profound** speech? Explain.

7. How would you **lull** a hissing cat?

8. What might make a road trip seem **relentless**? Explain.

9. What was the most **pivotal** scene in your favorite movie?

10. What would be **unprecedented** in the world of music? Why?

molten   If something is molten, it has been melted into a liquid by extreme heat.

murky   If something is murky, it is dark and difficult to see through.

volition   When you act on your own volition, you have the power and freedom to make your own decisions.

flushed   When you are flushed, your face turns red.

immobile   Something that is immobile can't be moved.

profound   A profound feeling or experience affects you deeply.

lull   If something lulls you, it makes you feel calm and sleepy.

relentless   Something that is relentless keeps going on and on for a very long time.

pivotal   A pivotal event is extremely important and can completely change the way things turn out.

unprecedented   If something is unprecedented, it has never happened before.

Take It Further

Complete these sentences on a separate piece of paper.

1. The cheese became **molten** when . . .

2. Because my fish tank was **murky** . . .

3. Sonia acts like she has no **volition** because . . .

4. Erika looked **flushed** after . . .

5. The robot remained **immobile** until . . .

6. The book was so **profound** that Rachel . . .

7. Jorge was **lulled** when Jenn told him . . .

8. Because the rain was **relentless**, we decided . . .

9. Todd's role in the play was **pivotal** because . . .

10. The mountain climber's trip was **unprecedented** because . . .

Explore It

You know the word *pivotal* by now, but how does it relate to the word *pivot*? A pivot is an object that stays in place while other things turn around it. A pivot is also the motion of keeping one foot on the floor and using the other foot to turn. Something pivotal is often described as a "turning point." If an event is pivotal, your whole life might metaphorically revolve around that event!

Think of something that could happen to you during the next year. It could be a huge, life-changing event (getting cast in a movie) or a normal, less exciting event (taking a nap). Write the event you've thought of on the board. When all your classmates' ideas are on the board, stand up and listen to your teacher read the list of events aloud. When you hear an event that you think would be pivotal, pivot by turning on one foot. The event that the most people pivot for is the most pivotal event!

Supplies for Spies

Real tools of the trade based on actual spy gadgets! Huge savings!

on sale now!

Something's Fishy

Need to pass along a package of pivotal information? Afraid to trust the local post office? Send your package safely by putting it in the belly of our Robotic Catfish. This frisky fake fish looks and moves exactly like the real thing! Simply place your top-secret package inside the catfish, set it free in a murky pond or stream, and let it swim toward your fellow secret agent.
$2,999.95

What's the Buzz?

Whether you're trying to learn important government secrets, or you just want to catch up on the latest gossip, our remote-controlled dragonfly is the perfect gadget for you! This bug holds a tiny listening device. Use the remote control to steer the dragonfly toward the secret conversation of your choice. Not for use in high winds. Batteries not included. Choose from green, blue, or black. Collect all three!
$700.00 each

Bird's-Eye View

If you need to take pictures from the air but don't want to attract attention in a noisy helicopter, we have a solution for you! Invest in our antique World War I-era Pigeon Cam. Strap the camera onto a pigeon and have it fly over enemy territory. The camera will take pictures automatically. Warning: Pigeon may fly away of its own volition. Keep away from enemies carrying birdseed.
Camera alone: $500.00
Camera and Pigeon Value Pack: $1,200.00

High-Tech Sneakers

Finally, a spy gadget that's both useful and fashionable! Record secret conversations with a click of your heels. A device that picks up and transmits sounds is built into the sole of our special Sneaky Shoe. Each shoe is imported from Russia and designed with your comfort in mind. Available in sizes 5–12.
$1,000.00 per pair

Stump Your Enemies

Lull your opponents into a false sense of security with this unique Tree Stump. It may not look like much, but a solar-powered gizmo that picks up radio signals is hidden inside. Unlike regular, immobile tree stumps, our award-winning version is lightweight and portable! Perfect for spies who live in forests. Why not buy several?
$3,499.99
Buy two, get one free! Limited time only.

Rev Up Your Writing

You've just read about average objects that have an unusual purpose. Invent a spy tool made from an everyday object and write an advertisement for it. Write about what your creation would be used for and how its similarity to an everyday object would make it useful. Use as many of the vocabulary words as possible but make sense.

Word Organizer

Copy this graphic organizer onto a separate piece of paper.

List words that are synonyms of *murky*. Write your answers in the Synonyms box. Use some of the words in this box to describe a murky day.

Then list words that are antonyms of *murky*. Write your answers in the Antonyms box. Use some of the words in this box to describe a nice day.

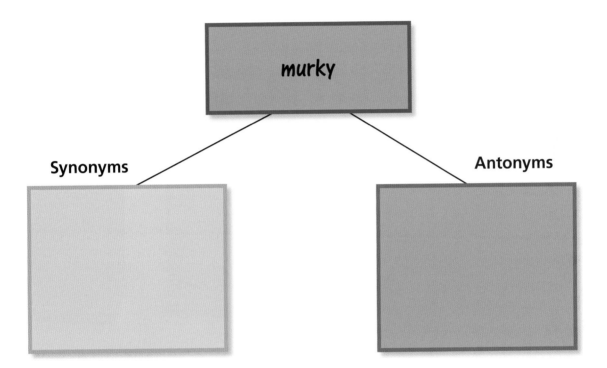

murky

Synonyms

Antonyms

Ask an ANCIENT GEOGRAPHER

Olivia

Ari

> Welcome to America's favorite quiz show, *Ask an Ancient Geographer!* I'm your host, Fred Magellan.

FRED: Welcome to America's favorite quiz show, *Ask an Ancient Geographer!* I'm your host, Fred Magellan. Our contestants today are 18-year-old Olivia Chavez from Pennsylvania and 16-year-old Ari Stotle, who's come here all the way from the distant past!

OLIVIA: What?

FRED: Let's start the game. For 100 points: *How many continents are there?*

OLIVIA: Seven.

FRED: I'm sorry. That's incorrect.

OLIVIA: No, it's not! There's South America, Antarctica . . .

ARI *(smugly)*: The correct answer is three: Asia, Europe, and Africa.

The Ancient World

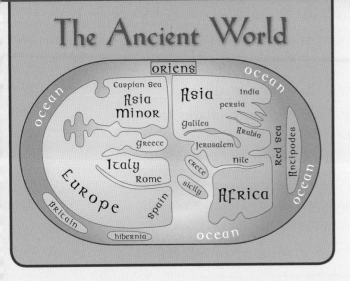

FRED: Correct!

OLIVIA *(flushed with anger)*: You're crazy!

FRED: I'm sorry, Olivia. According to our experts, your answer was wrong.

OLIVIA: Who exactly are these "experts"?

FRED: Ancient and medieval geographers, of course! Their theories may seem a little old-fashioned to you, but I prefer to think of them as profound.

OLIVIA: Oh . . .

FRED: Shall we move on? For 200 points: *If you sailed west from Ireland, where would you end up?*

OLIVIA *(nervously)*: Well, you'd probably end up in Canada.

FRED: Sorry, wrong again

ARI: Fred, as we all know, Ireland is at the very end of the world. There's nothing to the west except water. You might end up being turned into a puddle of molten flesh by a fire-breathing sea monster, though!

FRED: Correct! Nicely done, Ari. Don't worry, Olivia; there are still two questions left. For 300 points: *What creatures live on the opposite side of the world?*

OLIVIA: Do you mean Australia? I would normally say kangaroos and koalas, but I bet you're going to tell me I'm wrong.

ARI: I've heard fearsome tales of the monstrous creatures who live on the other side of the world. Their feet are opposite our own, which means that they must have feet growing out of their heads!

FRED: Yes! 300 points for Ari. Now, on to the final question. For a whopping 700 points: *Name something that orbits the earth.*

OLIVIA: The moon, of course!

FRED: Correct!

OLIVIA: It's about time!

ARI *(complaining relentlessly in the background)*: But Fred, she's forgetting the other stuff that orbits the earth! Like the sun, and all the planets, and the rings of fire and water that surround the earth, and . . .

FRED: That's all true, of course, Ari, but I'm afraid Olivia answered first. In an unprecedented come-from-behind victory, Olivia is today's champion! She's earned a free trip to the year 300 B.C. Thanks for watching, and see you next time on *Ask an Ancient Geographer!*

Rev Up Your Writing

During the game show, Olivia knew her answers were correct. Write about a time when you refused to change your mind about something when people said you were wrong. What happened as a result? Use as many of the vocabulary words as possible but make sense.

157

Can You Relate?

Copy this graphic organizer onto a separate piece of paper. Match the following words with their related vocabulary word. If a word relates to more than one vocabulary word, explain why.

conflagration   A conflagration is a large, destructive fire.
discomfit   If you feel discomfited, you feel uncomfortable or embarrassed.
phlegmatic   Someone who is phlegmatic is calm and hard to excite.
soporific   Something that is soporific can make you fall asleep.
torrid   If something is torrid, it is scorching hot.

molten	flushed	lull

In Your Own Words

Respond to one of the following prompts on a separate piece of paper. As you respond, use as many of the vocabulary words as possible. Be creative but make sense!

▶ Write about a time when you decided to try an activity because your friends or family members enjoyed it. What happened when you tried the activity for yourself?

▶ Imagine that you write an advice column. You've just received a letter from someone who's frustrated because she's not able to do something she's always dreamed of doing. Write a response giving your advice.

▶ Write about a topic of your choice.

VOCABULARY

molten
murky
volition
flushed
immobile
profound
lull
relentless
pivotal
unprecedented

Reflections on History in Missouri

By Constance
Urdang

Imagine a town that's haunted by things that happened long ago. There are some people who try to ignore the ghosts of history, but can anyone ever really escape the past?

My Arkansas

By Maya
Angelou

Reflections on History in Missouri

By Constance Urdang

This old house lodges no ghosts!
Those swaggering specters[1] who found their way
Across the Atlantic
Were left behind
With their old European grudges
In the farmhouses of New England
And Pennsylvania
Like so much jettisoned baggage
Too heavy
To lug over the Piedmont.[2]

The flatlands are inhospitable
To phantoms. Here
Shadows are sharp and arbitrary
Not mazy, obscure,
Cowering in corners
Behind scary old boots in a cupboard
Or muffled in empty coats, deserted
By long-dead cousins
(Who appear now and then
But only in photographs
Already rusting at the edges)—

Setting out in the creaking wagon
Tight-lipped,[3] alert to move on,
The old settlers had no room
For illusions.
Their dangers were real.
Now in the spare square house
Their great-grandchildren
Tidy away the past
Until the polished surfaces
Reflect not apparitions, pinched,
Parched,[4] craving, unsatisfied,
But only their own faces.

FOOTNOTES

[1] *specters:* spirits
[2] *the Piedmont:* part of the eastern United States near the Appalachian Mountains
[3] *tight-lipped:* not willing to speak
[4] *parched:* thirsty

My Arkansas

By Maya Angelou

There is a deep brooding
in Arkansas.
Old crimes like moss pend[1]
from poplar trees.
The sullen earth
is much too
red for comfort.

Sunrise seems to hesitate
and in that second
lose its
incandescent aim, and
dusk no more shadows
than the noon.
The past is brighter yet.

Old hates and
ante-bellum[2] lace, are rent[3]
but not discarded.
Today is yet to come
in Arkansas.
It writhes. It writhes in awful
waves of brooding.

FOOTNOTES

[1] *pend:* hang
[2] *ante-bellum:* pre-war;
in America, it refers
to the time before
the Civil War
[3] *rent:* torn

Explain Yourself

Answer each question on a separate piece of paper. Be sure to explain your answers.

1. Would you **jettison** a shirt you just bought? Explain.

2. Should you make an **arbitrary** decision about which college to attend? Explain.

3. What might make a dog **cower**? Explain.

4. What would you do if you thought you saw an **apparition**? Why?

5. What might cause you to have a **brooding** feeling? Why?

6. Would you want to be friends with a **sullen** person? Why or why not?

7. Would you want to wear an **incandescent** shirt? Explain.

8. What might happen in a football game that would make a player **writhe**?

9. What event in your life do you see differently when thinking about it in **retrospect**? Explain.

10. Would it be an **iniquity** if you were punished for something you didn't do? Explain.

VOCABULARY

jettison When you jettison something, you get rid of it because it is not needed or is causing a problem.

arbitrary An arbitrary action or decision is made without any good reason.

cower If a person or animal cowers, it crouches and moves back because it is afraid.

apparition An apparition is something that looks like a ghost.

brooding Brooding is used to describe a threatening and disturbing feeling.

sullen A person who is sullen is bad-tempered and unfriendly.

incandescent If something is incandescent, it shines brightly.

writhe When you writhe, you twist and turn because of extreme pain or shame.

retrospect When you think about something in retrospect, you think back on it and may change your opinion about it.

iniquity An iniquity is a situation or act that is unfair or wicked.

Take It Further

Complete these sentences on a separate piece of paper.

1. Todd **jettisoned** his plans because . . .

2. The family trip seemed **arbitrary** to Ming since . . .

3. The movie audience **cowered** when . . .

4. My friend said he saw an **apparition**, but it was only . . .

5. Akeem wouldn't stop **brooding** after he . . .

6. Kira seemed **sullen** to her classmates when she . . .

7. As we drove down the highway, we saw an **incandescent** . . .

8. Carlos started **writhing** after . . .

9. Fatima had a crush on Mic in elementary school, but in **retrospect** . . .

10. During the soccer game, Kim was upset with the **iniquity** of . . .

Explore It

Writhe **has a unique spelling and pronunciation—a silent** *w*! **This means that** *writhe* **sounds like it begins with an** *r*, **like the word** *retrospect*. **Can you think of any other words that share this trait?**

In a small group, use a dictionary to find five words that start with an *r* sound. Make sure at least two of the words begin with a silent *w*. Then write a tongue twister by using as many of the words as you can in a sentence that's really hard to say. Your tongue twister can be funny, but it must make sense, and it must contain the words *writhe* and *retrospect*. (Try saying, "The writhing worm retrospectively realized the robin's wrath" three times fast!) Challenge your classmates to repeat your tongue twister as fast as they can.

Hooray for Bollywood!

You've probably heard a lot about Hollywood—the celebrities, the palm trees, the endless stream of blockbuster movies. But how much do you know about Bollywood? Bollywood is a nickname for the film industry in India, which is based in Mumbai (formerly Bombay). Bollywood has its own set of movie stars, singers, and famous directors. More than 1,000 movies come out of Bollywood each year!

Bollywood films are rarely shown in the United States because most of them are in Hindi, an Indian language. Also, they're really long. American movies are usually less than two hours long. Bollywood films run at least three hours!

Bollywood films have other unique features, too. For instance, they're almost all musicals. Dancers in incandescent costumes and exotic makeup fill the screen. It's hard to feel sullen after seeing one of Bollywood's lively, over-the-top musical scenes.

Bollywood plots are just as vivid as the music. In an American movie, you wouldn't expect to see a thrilling car chase in a romantic comedy about a girl suffering an iniquity. A typical Bollywood film, however, isn't just about a romantic relationship or a thrilling event. It blends love, loss, action, and family issues into one brightly colored, delicious mixture. Slowly but surely, Bollywood films are coming to American audiences. Soon, your local movie theater might have Hindi titles posted beside the American titles!

So You Want to Be a Movie Star?

Things Teen Actors Need to Know

- Don't skip school! You may not have to sit in a classroom all day, but you can't jettison your education, either. Some actors are home-schooled or have a teacher come to the set.

- Stay focused! Most movies aren't taped from beginning to end. Instead, scenes are filmed in an order that can seem arbitrary, so it's easy to get confused about what's happening in your scene.

Rev Up Your Writing

If you had the chance to be involved in any movie you wanted, what kind of movie would it be? Write about a movie in which you would like to act. What role would you play? Use as many of the vocabulary words as you can but make sense.

165

Word Organizer

Copy this graphic organizer onto a separate piece of paper.

Sullen is near the cold end of the Word-O-Meter. Think of words that would be hotter or colder than *sullen*. Write your answers in the boxes. Explain your answers.

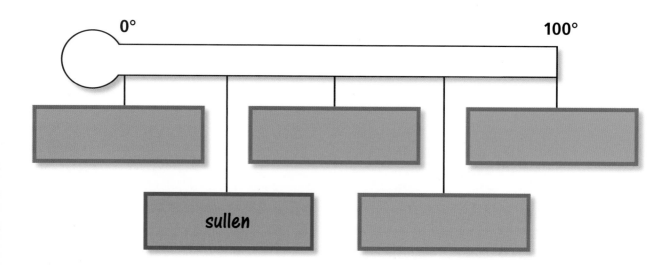

sullen

A young man once said that he wanted to be a great writer. He said, "I want to write things that will make people cry, scream, and become sullen." He now works for a computer company—writing error messages.

GREAT ESCAPE

FREEDOM SAIL

When Nazi soldiers invaded Denmark in 1940, a brooding atmosphere filled the country. In every country the Nazis invaded, they oppressed Jewish citizens. But the Danish people decided to help their Jewish neighbors. A secret group called the Resistance arranged to send all Jewish citizens across the Baltic Sea to safety in Sweden.

Families hid their Jewish friends and helped them get to the coast. Danish fishermen built secret compartments in their boats to hide people. They sailed back and forth to Sweden. When the Nazis found out, they sent soldiers with dogs to inspect fishing boats. The dogs were supposed to sniff out people who were hiding, but the Resistance had a solution for this, too. They gave the dogs handkerchiefs that contained special chemicals. After the dogs sniffed the handkerchiefs, they couldn't smell anything for a while, so they couldn't find any people hiding on the boats. Thanks to the Resistance, almost all 8,000 Jewish citizens of Denmark escaped safely.

167

AN APPARITION IN THE NIGHT SKY

From 1961 until 1989, an enormous wall divided the German city of Berlin into two parts, East Berlin and West Berlin. People in East Berlin didn't have as much freedom as people in West Berlin did, so many East Berliners tried to escape to West Berlin.

The Wetzel and Strelcyzk families decided to plan an escape that, in retrospect, seems almost too dangerous to attempt. They used a homemade hot air balloon to fly over the high, heavily guarded Berlin Wall. The balloon was sewn from scraps of cloth and filled with cooking gas heated with a flamethrower. An iron platform supported the gas canisters and all eight people on board.

On a windy September night in 1979, they launched the balloon in a meadow and floated toward the wall. The families cowered briefly when a searchlight hit their balloon, but it was too late for the East German troops to stop the balloon from crossing the wall. The families crash-landed a short time later into some West Berlin blackberry bushes. They may have been writhing from the blackberry thorns, but they were free.

Rev Up Your Writing

You've just read about two groups of people who made brave escapes to improve their lives. Write about a time when you or someone you know had to do something brave and daring. Use as many of the vocabulary words as you can but make sense.

Can You Relate?

Copy this graphic organizer onto a separate piece of paper. Match the following words with their related vocabulary word. If a word relates to more than one vocabulary word, explain why.

ethereal Something that is ethereal is light, airy, and hard to hold on to.

harbinger If something is a harbinger, it warns you that something is about to happen.

leery If you are leery of something, you feel suspicious of it and you don't trust it.

presentiment If you have a presentiment, you have a feeling about something before it happens.

spectral If something is spectral, it is very spooky.

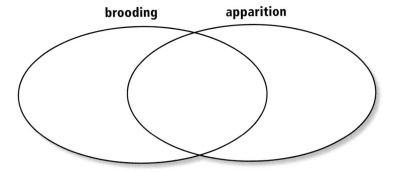

brooding   apparition

In Your Own Words

VOCABULARY

jettison
arbitrary
cower
apparition
brooding
sullen
incandescent
writhe
retrospect
iniquity

Respond to one of the following prompts on a separate piece of paper. As you respond, use as many of the vocabulary words as possible. Be creative but make sense!

▶ Write about the place where you live. How do you feel about it? What do you like or dislike about it?

▶ Write a humorous poem about an escape gone wrong.

▶ Write about a topic of your choice.

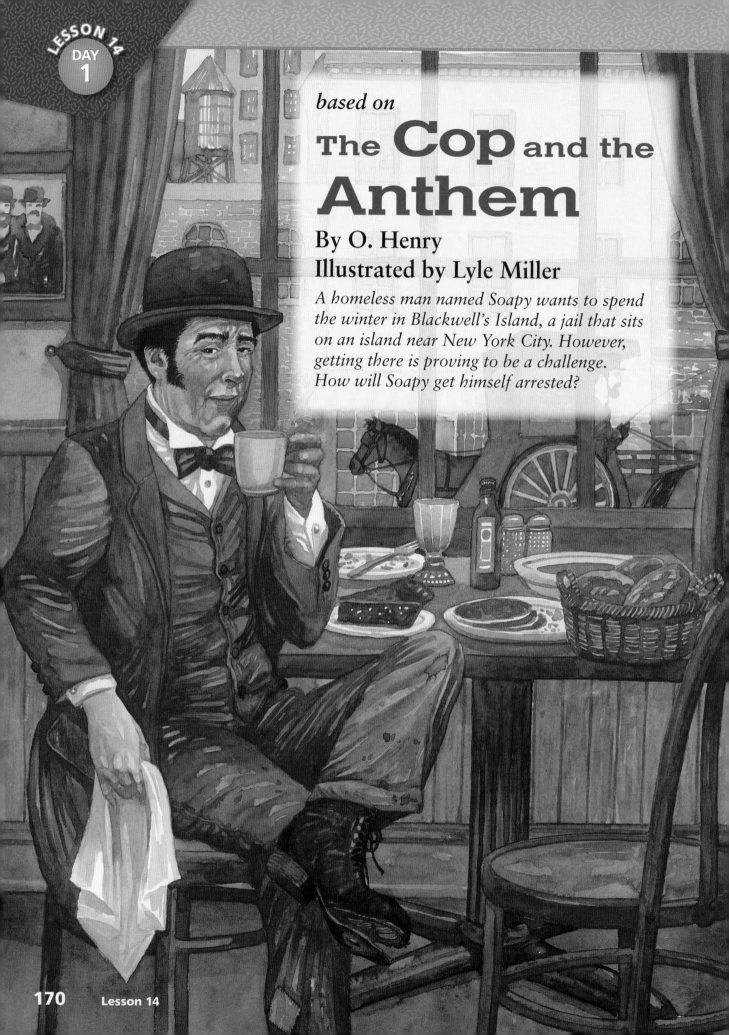

based on

The Cop and the Anthem

By O. Henry
Illustrated by Lyle Miller

A homeless man named Soapy wants to spend the winter in Blackwell's Island, a jail that sits on an island near New York City. However, getting there is proving to be a challenge. How will Soapy get himself arrested?

Soapy, having decided to go to the Island, at once set about accomplishing his desire. There were many easy ways of doing this. The pleasantest was to dine at some expensive restaurant, and then, after declaring that he is penniless, be handed over quietly and without uproar to a policeman. A helpful judge would do the rest.

Soapy left his bench and strolled out where Broadway and Fifth Avenue[1] flow together. Up Broadway he turned, and stopped at a glittering café.

Soapy had confidence in himself from the lowest button of his vest upward. He was shaven, and his coat was decent and his neat black bow-tie had been presented to him by a lady missionary on Thanksgiving Day. If he could reach a table in the restaurant unsuspected, success would be his. The portion of him that would show above the table would raise no doubt in the waiter's mind. A roasted mallard duck, thought Soapy, would be just the thing. The meat would leave him filled and happy for the journey to his winter refuge at the Island.

But as Soapy set foot inside the restaurant door, the headwaiter's eye fell upon his worn out trousers and old shoes. Strong and ready hands took him in silence and haste to the sidewalk, averting the ignoble fate of the threatened duck.

Soapy turned off Broadway. It seemed that his route to the coveted Island was not to be an easy one. Some other way of entering must be thought of.

At a corner of Sixth Avenue electric lights and cunningly displayed art behind plate-glass made a shop window clearly visible. Soapy took a cobblestone and dashed it through the glass. People came running round the corner, a policeman in the lead. Soapy stood still, with his hands in his pockets, and smiled at the sight of brass buttons.[2]

"Where's the man that done that?" inquired the officer excitedly.

"Don't you figure that I might have had something to do with it?" said Soapy, not without sarcasm, but friendly, as one greets good fortune.

FOOTNOTES
[1] *Broadway and Fifth Avenue:* two famous streets in New York City
[2] *brass buttons:* at the time of this story police officers wore brass buttons

The policeman's mind refused to accept Soapy even as a clue. "Men who smash windows do not remain to speak with police officers. They take to their heels."[3] The policeman saw a man halfway down the block running to catch a car. With drawn club he joined in the pursuit. Soapy, with disgust in his heart, walked off in disappointment, twice unsuccessful.

On the opposite side of the street was a restaurant of no obvious importance. It catered to large appetites and humble purses.[4] Into this place Soapy took his old shoes and telltale[5] trousers without challenge. At a table he sat and consumed beefsteak, flap-jacks, doughnuts, and pie. And then he mentioned to the waiter that he had no money.

"Now, get busy and call a cop," said Soapy. "And don't keep a gentleman waiting."

"No cop for youse," said the waiter, with a voice like butter cakes. "Hey, Con!"

Two waiters threw Soapy out of the restaurant neatly upon his left ear on the cold, hard pavement. He arose, joint by joint, and beat the dust from his clothes. Arrest seemed but a rosy dream. The Island seemed very far away. A policeman who stood before a drug store two doors away laughed and walked down the street.

A sudden fear seized Soapy that some dreadful enchantment had made him immune to arrest. The thought brought a little panic, and when he came upon another policeman lounging grandly in front of a theater he caught at the immediate straw[6] of "disorderly conduct."

On the sidewalk Soapy began to yell gibberish at the top of his harsh voice. He danced, howled, raved, and otherwise disturbed everyone around.

The policeman twirled his club, turned his back to Soapy and remarked to a citizen:

"'Tis one of them Yale lads celebratin' the goose egg[7] they give to the Hartford College. Noisy; but no harm. We've instructions to leave them be."

Disconsolate, Soapy stopped his racket. Would a policeman never lay hands on him? In his mind the Island seemed an unattainable Arcadia.[8] He buttoned his thin coat against the chilling wind.

FOOTNOTES

....

[3] *take to their heels:* run away

[4] *humble purses:* people with little money

[5] *telltale:* revealing

[6] *caught at the immediate straw:* had an idea

[7] *goose egg:* zero points scored

[8] *Arcadia:* peaceful place

Soapy peered down the street and saw a well-dressed man in a store. The man had set his silk umbrella by the door on entering the store. Soapy stepped inside, picked up the umbrella and sauntered off with it slowly. The man followed him hastily.

"My umbrella," the man said sternly.

"Oh, is it?" sneered Soapy, adding insult to petty theft. "Why don't you call a policeman? I took your umbrella! Why don't you call that cop on the corner?"

The umbrella owner slowed his steps. Soapy did the same, figuring his luck would run against him again. The policeman looked at the two curiously.

"Of course," said the umbrella man, "that is—well, you know how these things happen. I picked it up in a restaurant this morning—if you recognize it as yours—"

"Of course it's mine," Soapy said, angry his plan was foiled again.

The policeman left to escort a tall blonde across the busy street.

Soapy walked eastward through a street damaged by improvements. He hurled the umbrella into a hole and muttered against the men who wear helmets and carry clubs. Because he wanted to fall into their clutches, they seemed to regard him as a king who could do no wrong.

But on an unusually quiet corner Soapy came to a standstill. Here was an old, quaint church. Through one violet-stained window a soft light glowed where the organist played, making sure of his mastery of the coming Sabbath anthem. From there drifted out to Soapy's ears sweet music that caught and held him motionless.

The anthem that the organist played cemented Soapy to the iron fence of the church, for he had known it well in the days when his life contained such things as mothers and roses and ambitions and friends and immaculate[9] thoughts and collars.

Soapy's receptive state of mind and the influences about the old church brought a sudden and wonderful change in his soul. He viewed with swift horror the pit into which he had tumbled, the degraded days, unworthy desires, dead hopes, wrecked faculties,[10] and evil motives that made up his existence.

FOOTNOTES
[9] *immaculate:* pure
[10] *faculties:* talents or capabilities

His heart responded thrillingly to this new mood. An instantaneous and strong impulse moved him to battle with his desperate fate. He would pull himself up; he would make a man of himself again; he would conquer the evil that had taken over. There was time; he was still young; he would awaken his old eager ambitions and pursue them without faltering. Those sweet organ notes had changed his heart. Tomorrow he would go into the busy downtown and find work. A clothing store had once offered him a position. He would go there tomorrow and ask for the job. He would be somebody in the world. He would—

Soapy felt a hand laid on his arm. He looked quickly into the broad face of a policeman.

"What are you doin' here?" asked the officer.

"Nothin'," said Soapy.

"Then come along," said the policeman.

"Three months on the Island," said the Judge in the Police Court the next morning.

Explain Yourself

VOCABULARY

Answer each question on a separate piece of paper. Be sure to explain your answers.

1. How might you **avert** an argument between two of your friends?

2. Would you share a secret with an **ignoble** person? Explain.

3. Would a well-dressed teenager **covet** designer jeans? Why or why not?

4. Do rainy days make you feel **disconsolate**? Why or why not?

5. Would you want to visit a library where Internet access is **unattainable**? Why or why not?

6. Would you describe the town you live in as **quaint**? Explain.

7. Would you want your parents to be **receptive** to your opinions? Explain.

8. How would you feel if somebody **degraded** you? Why?

9. Would you want to **loiter** at the library? Why or why not?

10. Would you consider playing violent video games an **illicit** activity?

avert   When you avert something, you keep it from happening.

ignoble   Something that is ignoble is dishonorable and has a bad reputation.

covet   If you covet something, you want it for yourself.

disconsolate   A disconsolate person is so sad he or she can't be cheered up.

unattainable   Something that is unattainable is impossible to get.

quaint   If something is quaint, it is old-fashioned and charming.

receptive   Someone who is receptive is open to new ideas and experiences.

degrade   If you degrade someone or something, you damage its value or reputation.

loiter   When you loiter somewhere, you stay there without any good reason.

illicit   An illicit activity is illegal or not allowed.

Take It Further

Complete these sentences on a separate piece of paper.

1. Kitana **averted** a loss for her team by . . .
2. Shelby led a protest against the **ignoble** . . .
3. Angelo told Koshi that he **coveted** . . .
4. Jared became **disconsolate** when he read about . . .
5. Winning the gold medal was **unattainable** for the figure skater after . . .
6. People described the hotel as **quaint** because . . .
7. Olivia was surprised when her sister was **receptive** to . . .
8. Comedians **degrade** celebrities by . . .
9. To keep people from **loitering**, the store owner . . .
10. Because of Maxwell's **illicit** behavior, he . . .

Explore It

Homophones, or words that are pronounced the same but spelled differently, can be confusing. The word *elicit* is a homophone for the word *illicit*. It's important to know the difference between these words. Your computer's spell check program can't tell you whether a word is misused; it can only tell you if it is misspelled.

illicit
If something is illicit, it is illegal or not allowed.

elicit
When you elicit a response from someone, you cause that person to react to something you have done or said.

Working with a partner, use the following homophones correctly in your own quote or riddle. Be prepared to share your quotes with the class. Example: "Illicit ways don't elicit praise."

1. idol, idle
2. principal, principle
3. morning, mourning
4. allowed, aloud
5. compliment, complement
6. site, cite, sight

Dodgeball Goes Pro!

Remember that large rubber ball that stung you at recess? Yeah, dodgeball. Well, it's not just a quaint kid's game anymore. With its own professional league and world championship, dodgeball is a real sport. OK, it might not be quite as popular as football or basketball, but this game of fast throws, flying leaps, and quick dodges is taking the nation by storm.

In a professional dodgeball game, two teams throw rubber balls at each other, trying to hit the other team's players while avoiding getting hit themselves. Dodgeball moves at a lightning pace, and there's no time for loitering. If you get bored during never-ending games of baseball, dodgeball may be the perfect sport for you.

If you're interested in playing professional dodgeball, you can try out for four official teams: the Wisconsin Ions, Minnesota Blur, Texas Shade, and New York Empire. But don't worry if your dodgeball skills aren't up to professional standards yet. Amateur teams play across the country and compete in the annual Dodgeball World Championship.

Want to try dodgeball for yourself? Use the information on the next page to form a team at your school.

Rules of the Game

The Equipment
Dodgeball is played with six rubber-covered foam balls.

The Field
A dodgeball field is rectangular and can be indoors or outdoors. The field is divided by a center line, like a soccer field or basketball court. Each team has to stay on its own side of the field.

The Teams
At least 12 players, 6 per team.

The Game
Three throwers on either team grab one of three balls from their side of the centerline. They step behind their attack line and throw the balls at opposing players.

- If a defender is hit with a ball below the shoulders, he or she is out.
- If a defender catches a ball, the thrower is out.
- When your team gets all the other team's players out, your team wins!

Stuff to Avoid

- Stalling, or keeping all six balls on your side of the court, is illicit!
- Aiming the ball above the shoulders is also against the rules.
- Don't be a wimp! If a player degrades himself by running off the field to avert a hit, he's out of the game.

Rev Up Your Writing

Think about the games you enjoyed playing as a child and the games you enjoy playing now. Write a short essay that explains how they are alike and how they are different. Use as many vocabulary words as possible but make sense.

Word Organizer

Copy this graphic organizer onto a separate piece of paper.

List activities that you would be receptive to in the top half of the Word Wheel. List activities that you would not be receptive to in the bottom half.

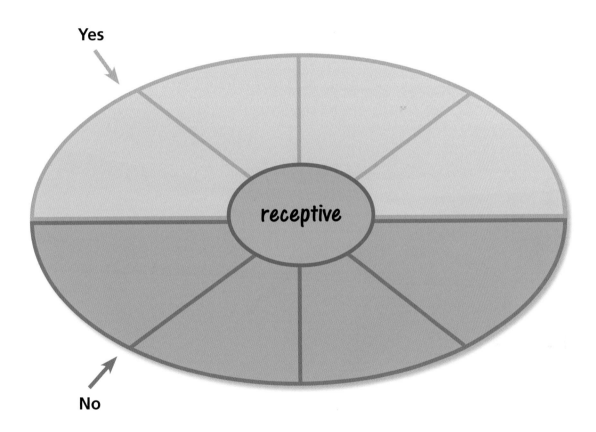

Yes

receptive

No

The World's WEIRDEST Race

The annual Kinetic Sculpture Race is held every May in northern California. People from all over the country turn recycled bike parts, lawn mower parts, and auto parts into works of art and racing machines. The race usually lasts for three days and the machines have to travel over water, mud, city streets, and sand. Victory may seem unattainable, but riders must stick to pedaling or pushing—no engines are allowed!

5/24
Today we left for Arcata, California. The Kinetic Sculpture Race is only four days away!

5/26
Laura called to thank me again for agreeing to race the Giant Eye she designed for the kinetic sculpture race. I have to admit that I wasn't too receptive to driving it at first. I mean, I worked all summer to build my Leapin' Lizard with hopes of winning the coveted Kinetic Sculptor Trophy. But it would be ignoble to bail on Laura while she's stuck at home with bronchitis.

5/27
I took the old eye for a practice spin today. I never thought driving a giant eyeball could be so much fun! It uses gears from a ten-speed bike and turns corners with ease. And there's even a radio! I should have known Laura would find a way to put music in that thing.

5/30
The race was a blast! Although I had to tell Laura that we came in fifth place, she wasn't disconsolate at all. The Giant Eye actually got an honorable mention in the design contest! It was the only racer with music!
    This year's designs were the coolest ever! There were huge cats and fish and a 10-foot-long two-headed dragon. My friend Maury's racer was a hedgehog wearing a bandana. And I can't get over the gigantic nose with green snot hanging out. Nasty!

5/31
We're going home today. I can't wait to show Laura the pictures! Plus, I've already got a few tricks up my sleeve for next year's race.

Rev Up Your Writing

You've just read a travelogue—a diary of what a person sees on a trip. Write a travelogue about a person who goes on an unusual road trip. Use as many vocabulary words as possible but make sense.

Can You Relate?

Copy this graphic organizer onto a separate piece of paper. Match the following words with their related vocabulary word. If a word relates to more than one vocabulary word, explain why.

circumvent   If you circumvent something, you avoid it.
perjure   If you perjure yourself, you tell a lie.
sabotage   If you sabotage something, you try to ruin it on purpose.
scoundrel   A scoundrel is a dishonorable person.
usurp   If you usurp another person's position, you try to take it by force.

ignoble	covet	avert

In Your Own Words

Respond to one of the following prompts on a separate piece of paper. As you respond, use as many of the vocabulary words as possible. Be creative but make sense!

▶ Write about a time when you tried to get the attention of someone you liked or respected. What did you do? Did you succeed or fail? How do you feel about the experience now?

▶ Make up your own extreme sport. Write a how-to guide explaining the rules of the game.

▶ Write about a topic of your choice.

VOCABULARY

avert
ignoble
covet
disconsolate
unattainable
quaint
receptive
degrade
loiter
illicit

My TWO Dads

By Marie G. Lee • Illustrated by Winson Trang

Marie Lee thinks she's just a normal, American girl with a normal, American dad. On a family trip to Korea, however, Marie discovers that her dad isn't exactly who she thought he was.

I am a first-generation Korean-American. On my first trip to Korea at age twenty-six, I found that I had two fathers. One was the Dad I'd always known, but the second was a Korean father I'd never seen before—one surprising and familiar at the same time, like my homeland.

I was born and raised in the Midwest, and to me, my Dad was like anyone else's. He taught my brothers to play baseball, fixed the garage door, and pushed the snowblower on chilly February mornings. If there was anything different about him, to my child's eyes, it was that he was a doctor.

Growing up, my siblings and I rarely came into contact with our Korean heritage. Mom and Dad spoke Korean only when they didn't want us to know what they were saying. We didn't observe Korean customs, except for not wearing shoes in the house, which I always assumed was plain common sense. I'd once seen a photograph of Dad in a traditional Korean costume, and I remember thinking how odd those clothes made him look.

With my parents' tacit encouragement, I "forgot" that I was Korean. I loved pizza and macaroni and cheese, but I had never so much as touched a slice of kimchi.[1] All my friends, including my boyfriend, were Caucasian. And while I could explain in detail everything I thought was wrong with Ronald Reagan's policies, I had to strain to remember the name of Korea's president.

Attempting to learn the Korean language, *hangukmal*, a few years ago was a first step in atoning for my past indifference. I went into it feeling smug because of my fluency in French and German, but learning Korean knocked me for a loop.[2] This was a language shaped by Confucian[3] rules of reverence, where the speaker states her position (humble, equal, superior) in relation to the person she is addressing. Simultaneously humbling myself and revering the person with whom I was speaking seemed like a painful game of verbal Twister. To further complicate the process, I found there are myriad titles of reverence, starting with the highest, *sansengnim*, which loosely means "teacher/doctor," down to the ultra-specific, such as *waysukmo*, "wife of mother's brother."

FOOTNOTES

1 *kimchi:* a spicy Korean vegetable dish
2 *knocked me for a loop:* was surprisingly difficult
3 *Confucian:* based on the teachings of the ancient Chinese philosopher Confucius

Armed, then, with a year's worth of extension-school classes, a list of polite phrases and titles, and a Berlitz[4] tape in my Walkman, I was as ready as I'd ever be to travel with my family to Korea last year.

When we arrived at Kimpo Airport in Seoul,[5] smiling relatives funneled us into the customs line for *wayguksalam,* "foreigners." I was almost jealous watching our Korean flight attendants breeze through the line for *hanguksalam,* "Korean nationals." With whom did I identify more—the flight attendants or the retired white couple behind us, with their Bermuda shorts and Midwestern accents? My American passport stamped me as an alien in a land where everyone looked like me.

I got my first glimpse of my second father when we began trying to hail cabs in downtown Seoul. Because the government enforces low taxi fares, the drivers have developed their own system of picking up only individual passengers, then packing more in, to increase the per-trip profit. The streets are clogged not only with traffic but also with desperately gesticulating[6] pedestrians and empty taxis.

Even my mother was stymied by the cab-hailing competition. When Mom and I traveled alone, cabs zoomed blithely[7] past us. When we finally got one, the driver would shut off his meter, brazenly charge us triple the usual fare and ignominiously dump us somewhere not very close to our destination.

But traveling with Dad was different. He would somehow stop a taxi with ease, chitchat with the driver (using very polite language), then shovel us all in. Not only would the cabbie take us where we wanted to go, but some of the usually taciturn drivers would turn into garrulous philosophers.

I began to perceive the transformation of my father from American dad to functioning urban Korean. When we met with relatives, I noticed how Dad's conversational Korean moved easily between the respect he gave his older sister to the joviality with which he addressed Mom's younger cousin. My brother Len and I and our Korean cousins, however, stared shyly and mutely at each other.

FOOTNOTES

[4] *Berlitz:* a school for language instruction
[5] *Seoul:* the capital of South Korea
[6] *gesticulating:* moving your arms or hands to help communicate
[7] *blithely:* casually and carelessly

Keeping company with relatives eased my disorientation, but not my alienation. Korea is the world's most racially and culturally homogeneous[8] country, and although I was of the right race, I felt culturally shut out. It seemed to me that Koreans were pushy, even in church. When they ate, they slurped and inhaled their food so violently that at least once during every meal, someone would have a sputtering fit of coughing.

Watching my father "turn Korean" helped me as I tried to embrace the culture. Drinking *soju* in a restaurant in the somewhat seedy Namdaemun area, he suddenly lit into[9] a story of the time when Communists from North Korea confiscated his parents' assets.[10] Subsequently, he became a medical student in Seoul, where each day he ate a sparse breakfast at his sister's house, trekked across towering Namsan Mountain (visible from our room in the Hilton), and studied at Seoul National University until night, when he would grab a few hours of sleep in the borrowed bed of a friend who worked the night shift.

I have always lived in nice houses, gone on trips, and never lacked for pizza money. But as my father talked, I could almost taste the millet-and-water gruel he subsisted[11] on while hiding for months in cellars during the North Korean invasion of Seoul. Suddenly, I was able to feel the pain of the Korean people, enduring one hardship after another: Japanese colonial rule, North Korean aggression, and dependence on American military force. For a brief moment, I discerned[12] the origins of the noble, sometimes harsh, Korean character. Those wizened[13] women who pushed past me at church were there only because they had fought their way to old age. Those noises people made while eating began to sound more celebratory than rude.

And there were other things I saw and was proud of. When we visited a cemetery, I noticed that the headstones were small and unadorned, except for a few with small, pagoda-shaped "hats" on them. The hats (*chinsa*), Dad told me, were from a time when the country's leaders awarded "national Ph.D.'s," the highest civilian honor.

FOOTNOTES

8 *homogeneous:* all the same
9 *lit into:* started telling
10 *assets:* money and property
11 *subsisted:* survived
12 *discerned:* understood
13 *wizened:* wrinkled

"Your great-grandfather has one of those on his grave," Dad mentioned casually. I began to admire a people who place such high value on hard work and scholarship. Even television commercials generally don't promote leisure pursuits, such as vacations or Nintendo, but instead proclaim the merits of "super duper vitamin pills" to help you study longer and work harder.

After two weeks, as we prepared to return to the U.S., I still in many ways felt like a stranger in Korea. While I looked the part of a native, my textbook Korean was robotic, and the phrases I was taught—such as, "Don't take me for a five-won plane ride"—were apparently very dated. I tried to tell my Korean cousins an amusing anecdote: in the Lotte department store in Seoul, I asked for directions to the restroom and was directed instead to the stereo section. But the story, related once in English and once in halting Korean, became hopelessly lost in the translation.

Dad decided he would spend an extra week in Korea, savoring a culture I would never fully know, even if I took every Berlitz course I could afford. When I said goodbye to him, I saw my Korean father; but I knew that come February, my American dad would be back out in our driveway, stirring up a froth of snow with his big yellow snowblower.

Explain Yourself

Answer each question on a separate piece of paper. Be sure to explain your answers.

1. What sorts of things are **tacit** between you and your best friend? Explain.

2. What might a professional athlete have to **atone** for? Explain.

3. Would you want to receive **myriad** cards on Valentine's Day? Why or why not?

4. Would you be **stymied** by a difficult math equation? Why or why not?

5. What would you do if you saw someone **brazenly** litter? Explain.

6. If your favorite celebrity did something **ignominious**, how would you react? Why?

7. Would you want to attend a party full of **taciturn** guests? Why or why not?

8. Would you want to go to the movies with a **garrulous** person? Why or why not?

9. Would winning a medal at the Olympics fill you with **apathy**? Explain.

10. What object would be **incongruous** in outer space? Explain.

VOCABULARY

tacit Something that is tacit is understood or agreed upon without having to talk about it.

atone When you atone for something that you did wrong, you do something to make up for it.

myriad If you have myriad things, you have a very large number of them.

stymie If you are stymied by something, you just don't know what to do about it.

brazenly When you do something brazenly, you do it openly even though you know it's wrong.

ignominiously If you behave ignominiously, you do something that is shameful and disgraceful.

taciturn Taciturn people may seem unfriendly because they don't talk very much.

garrulous Garrulous people talk a lot, especially about unimportant things.

apathy Apathy is a lack of interest in or enthusiasm about anything.

incongruous If something is incongruous, it seems strange because it is out of place.

Take It Further

Complete these sentences on a separate piece of paper.

1. During the hockey game, Paolo and I had a **tacit** understanding that . . .
2. Tamika wanted to **atone** for . . .
3. There were **myriad** places to visit during our family trip, so . . .
4. Eric's dream of being a rock star was **stymied** when . . .
5. Harmony's cat **brazenly** . . .
6. While at her cousin's wedding, Mariko **ignominiously** . . .
7. Ivan seems **taciturn** in class, but after school he . . .
8. Omar was so **garrulous** during English class that . . .
9. Because Jon was **apathetic** about football, . . .
10. Cate looked **incongruous** at the beach because . . .

LESSON 15
DAY
4

Explore It

You know the word *ignominious* by now, but did you know that some of its synonyms have slightly different meanings? If you say that someone is acting ignominiously, you certainly aren't giving that person a compliment. That's because the word *ignominious* has a very negative connotation. This means that when you use it, you're suggesting that you're talking about something very bad. *Ignominious* has a lot of synonyms, but some of these words' connotations are worse than others. Is it worse to be improper or disgusting?

Have each person in your group write one of the synonyms of *ignominious* listed below on a piece of paper and then draw a picture illustrating the word. Holding your piece of paper, arrange all the people in your group in a straight line. The order of the lineup depends on the word each person is holding—the word with the most positive connotation should be at the front, and the word with the most negative connotation should be at the back. There may be more than one correct answer. Now pretend your teacher is the word *ignominious*. Where in your line would *ignominious* go?

embarrassing, pitiful, improper, disgusting, mean, bad, shameful, shocking

Plan Your Dream Vacation!

Venezia

Visit VENICE

Come for the culture and romance. Stay for the water.

Do you love the ocean? If so, you'll love Venice, Italy! Why spend your vacation near the water when you can come to Venice and stay in the water?

Unlike most other cities, Venice is truly "on the move"—it's sinking into the Adriatic Sea! But don't let the rising ocean stymie your vacation plans. Think of the thrill you'll feel as you pull on your flippers and swim across historic St. Mark's Square during high tide. You'll make friends with everyone you meet on the street, from the garrulous locals to the more taciturn sea creatures.

This lovely location may be available for a limited time only, so book your tickets today!

SEE SKY CITY

In Sky City, you've got nowhere to go but up.

If you're feeling sad, a vacation might be just what you need to lift your spirits. When you visit Japan's Sky City 1000, you'll feel like you're on top of the world!

Although it's not yet built, Sky City will be a vertical city extending over 3,000 feet into the air. Its towers will contain myriad apartments, offices, stores, schools, and maybe even a sports stadium. The city will even include the things you love most about the outside world: trees, flowers, and grass.

Other cities may say they're the world's top travel destination, but Sky City will literally tower above them all. Why suffer the ignominy of vacationing anywhere else?

Rev Up Your Writing

You've just read about two unique cities. Write about what makes your town or city unique. What would you say to tourists who were interested in visiting your city? Use as many of the vocabulary words as possible but make sense.

191

Word Organizer

Copy this graphic organizer onto a separate piece of paper.

List things that would be incongruous in the desert and write your answers under the desert column. Then list things that would be incongruous at the South Pole and write your answers under the South Pole column. Explain your answers.

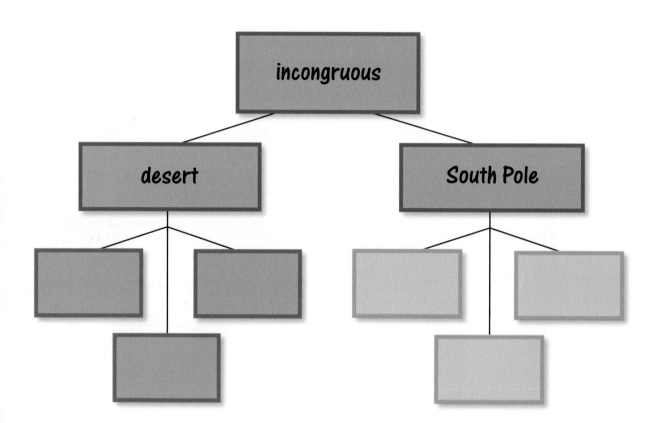

ASK THE MAD SCIENTIST:
THE TRUTH ABOUT TIME TRAVEL

Dear Mad Scientist,

I feel out of place in the 21st century. Is there any way I can travel through time and go somewhere more exciting?

—**Tick Tock in Tampa**

Dear Tick,

The idea of time travel is enough to excite even the most apathetic traveler. But will it ever be a reality?

Surprisingly, the answer may be yes!

No, I'm not telling you a brazen lie. Although most people share a tacit belief that time travel won't ever exist outside of sci-fi movies, scientists think that time travel to the future is possible.

If you want to travel to the future right now, you'll need a very fast spaceship. According to the laws of physics, things that travel very fast don't age as quickly as things that are traveling more slowly. This means that if you flew through outer space for 20 years at close to the speed of light, you'd return to find that 46 years had passed on Earth. You would have traveled 26 years forward in time!

Unfortunately, no one has come up with a practical time-travel machine yet, so your escape to the year 3000 will have to wait. Until then, ignore people who say time travel is impossible. In a few years, they may find themselves atoning for their comments!

—**The Mad Scientist**

Which Century Do You Belong In?

Do you think you were born in the wrong time? When time travel becomes possible, you can just pack up and go wherever—and whenever—you want! But which time is perfect for you? This quiz will help you determine your ideal time-travel destination.

1

If you could wear anything to school, what would it be?
- a) a suit of armor
- b) a stylish hat and leather boots
- c) a suit that changes color with your moods
- d) jeans and a T-shirt—nothing too incongruous

2

What's your favorite kind of music?
- a) classical music or anything sung by monks
- b) guitar music played by the campfire
- c) whatever's on the MP3 chip implanted in your brain
- d) pop, rock, hip-hop, or rap

3

Which sport would you most like to try?
- a) sword fighting
- b) horseback riding
- c) anti-gravity ball
- d) snowboarding

4

Which after-school activity sounds coolest?
- a) exploring a castle
- b) searching for gold nuggets
- c) hanging out with your clone
- d) playing a video game with your friends

If you chose:	Your ideal time-travel destination is:
mostly As	medieval Europe!
mostly Bs	the 19th-century American west!
mostly Cs	the future!
mostly Ds	now! Stay at home and enjoy the present.

Rev Up Your Writing

You've just read about time travel. If you could travel to any time and place, where would you go and why? Describe what you would want to experience in that time and place. Use as many of the vocabulary words as possible but make sense.

Can You Relate?

Copy this graphic organizer onto a separate piece of paper. Match the following words with their related vocabulary word. If a word relates to more than one vocabulary word, explain why.

divulge If you divulge information, you tell it to other people.
introvert If you are an introvert, you're quiet and shy.
orator An orator is someone who gives public speeches.
paltry If you have a paltry amount of something, you have a very small amount of it.
rhetoric If you have a talent for rhetoric, you are good at using words to persuade people or to exaggerate.

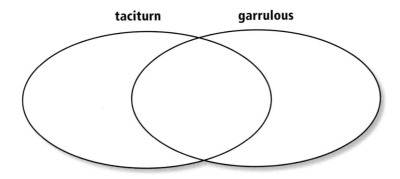

taciturn   garrulous

In Your Own Words

Respond to one of the following prompts on a separate piece of paper. As you respond, use as many of the vocabulary words as possible. Be creative but make sense!

▶ Write about a few of your family's traditions. Does your family eat special foods, celebrate certain holidays, or speak another language? What makes your family unique?

▶ Imagine that you are one of your ancestors who lived 100 years ago. Write a page from your autobiography. Where and when did you live? What was your life like? What challenges did you face?

▶ Write about a topic of your choice.

VOCABULARY

tacit
atone
myriad
stymie
brazenly
ignominiously
taciturn
garrulous
apathy
incongruous

based on **The**

Masque
of the
Red Death

By Edgar Allan Poe
Illustrated by Hrana Janto

*When a deadly disease known as the Red Death
spreads through the land, Prince Prospero
takes action to keep his friends and himself safe.
Will it be enough to hold back the Red Death?*

A plague known as the "Red Death" had long devastated the country. No pestilence[1] had ever been so deadly, or so hideous. There were sharp pains, and sudden dizziness, and then profuse bleeding at the pores. People died within a half hour of contracting the disease.

But Prince Prospero was happy and fearless. After he lost half the people in his kingdom, he called a thousand friends from among the knights and ladies of his court, and with them withdrew into the deep, impermeable seclusion of one of his abbeys. A strong, tall wall surrounded it, and this wall had gates of iron. After everyone had entered, the courtiers[2] brought furnaces and hammers and welded shut the bolts of the gates. No one would be allowed in or out, for any reason. The external world could take care of itself. The prince had provided all the appliances of pleasure. There were buffoons,[3] ballet-dancers, and musicians. All these—and safety—were within. Without was the Red Death.

It was toward the close of the fifth or sixth month of this seclusion, and while the pestilence still raged, that Prince Prospero entertained his thousand friends at a masked ball of the most unusual magnificence.

The masquerade was held in seven rooms. In the middle of each wall was a tall and narrow Gothic window of stained glass whose color varied to match the decorations of the room. The room at the eastern extremity was decorated in blue—and vividly blue were its windows. The second room was purple in its ornaments and tapestries, and here the windowpanes were purple. The third was green throughout. The fourth was furnished and lighted with orange—the fifth with white—the sixth with violet. The seventh apartment was shrouded in black velvet tapestries that hung all over the ceiling and down the walls, falling in heavy folds upon a carpet of the same material and color. But in this room only, the color of the windows failed to match the decorations. The windowpanes here were scarlet—a deep blood color. In this room the effect of the fire-light that streamed upon the dark hangings through the blood-tinted panes was ghastly in the extreme and produced so wild a look that there were few at the party bold enough to set foot within.

FOOTNOTES
1 *pestilence:* disease
2 *courtiers:* assistants
3 *buffoons:* clowns

It was in this room, also, that there stood against the western wall a gigantic ebony clock. Its pendulum swung to and fro with a dull, heavy, monotonous clang. When the clock struck the hour, it created such a loud, disturbing sound that, each time, the musicians of the orchestra paused, which brought the dancers to a stop and signaled a pause in the entire party. While the chimes of the clock rang, those having fun grew pale and passed their hands over their brows as if confused. But when the clock's echoes ceased, a light laughter could be heard in the crowd at once; the musicians looked at each other and smiled, as if laughing at their own nervousness. They made whispering vows that the next chiming of the clock would not make them feel the same way.

But, in spite of these things, it was a magnificent revel. The tastes of the duke were peculiar. He had a fine eye for colors and effects. His plans were bold and fiery, and his conceptions glowed with ferocious intensity.

He had directed, in great part, the embellishments of the seven rooms, and it was his own guiding taste that had given costume ideas to the masqueraders. There were figures with mismatched limbs and measurements. There were madman fashions. There were much of the beautiful, much of the wanton, much of the bizarre, something of the terrible, and not a little of that which might have caused disgust.

All but the black room were densely crowded, and in them the heart of life beat feverishly. The revel went whirlingly on, until the clock struck midnight. Again the music ceased; the waltzers were quieted, and there was an uneasy cessation[4] of all things as before. But now before the last echoes of the last chime had sunk into silence, many people had become aware of the presence of a masked figure. The rumor of this new guest spread itself whisperingly around, and there arose a buzz, or murmur, expressive of surprise and disapproval—then, finally, of terror, of horror, and of disgust.

In such a party, an ordinary costume wouldn't have created such a sensation. But the figure in question had gone beyond the bounds of even the prince's wild taste. The figure was tall and gaunt, and dressed as if he had risen from the grave. The mask that concealed the face so nearly resembled the face of a stiffened corpse that one could scarcely detect the difference. And yet all this might have been accepted, if not approved, by the revelers, but the costume had gone so far as to display the symptoms of the Red Death. The costume itself was covered in blood—as was the man's mask.

FOOTNOTES
....
[4] *cessation:* stopping

When the eyes of Prince Prospero fell upon this image, he first shuddered in either terror or distaste; but then, his face reddened with rage.

"Who dares insult us with this mockery? Seize him and unmask him—so that we may know whom we have to hang at sunrise!"

The prince stood in the blue room with a group of pale courtiers by his side. At first, as he spoke, there was a slight rushing movement toward the intruder, who was starting to walk towards the prince. But no one put forth a hand to seize him, so that, unimpeded, he passed within a yard of the prince. The vast group shrank away from the centers of the rooms to the walls, allowing the masked figure to make his way uninterruptedly from the blue chamber to the purple—through the purple to the green—through the green to the orange—through this again to the white—and on to the violet. It was then, however, that Prince Prospero, maddening with rage and the shame of his own momentary cowardice, rushed through the six rooms in pursuit. Just as he reached the retreating figure, he drew his dagger. The intruder turned suddenly and confronted his pursuer. There was a sharp cry—and the dagger dropped gleaming upon the black carpet, onto which, instantly afterwards, Prince Prospero fell dead. Then the revelers threw themselves into the black room and, grabbing the intruder, gasped in horror at finding no one behind the corpse-like mask.

And now everyone knew that the intruder was the Red Death. He had come quietly in the night, and one by one he killed the revelers, soaking the halls and rooms with blood. The life of the ebony clock went out, and darkness and decay and the Red Death held power over all.

Explain Yourself

VOCABULARY

Answer each question on a separate piece of paper. Be sure to explain your answers.

1. Would you want to have a **profuse** amount of homework? Explain.

2. Would you expect water to leak from something that is **impermeable**? Why or why not?

3. When might someone need to be **shrouded**? Explain.

4. Would a **monotonous** TV show hold your interest? Why or why not?

5. Why would you not want to have a **revel** at your house? Explain.

6. What **embellishments** would you like to add to your room? Why?

7. What would you do if you saw your friend do something **wanton**? Explain.

8. Would you want to adopt a **gaunt** kitten? Why or why not?

9. If someone in your class had an **insidious** cold, what might happen? Explain.

10. Would wearing a **garish** outfit to school impress your friends? Why or why not?

profuse If there is a profuse amount of something, there is a lot of it.

impermeable If something is impermeable, it is impossible to enter it or break through it.

shrouded If someone or something has been shrouded, it has been covered, usually with a cloth.

monotonous When something is monotonous, it is very boring because it never changes.

revel A revel is a loud celebration.

embellishment An embellishment is a decoration that is added to something to make it seem more attractive.

wanton A wanton action causes harm to someone or something on purpose without any reason.

gaunt A person who is gaunt is very skinny and unhealthy looking.

insidious You use insidious to describe something harmful that spreads slowly without being noticed.

garish When something is garish, it is so flashy and colorful that it's ugly.

Take It Further

Complete these sentences on a separate piece of paper.

1. Because José had a **profuse** amount of money, he . . .

2. Paul thought the wall was **impermeable**, so he was surprised when . . .

3. The furniture in the old house was **shrouded** because . . .

4. Because the lecture was **monotonous**, Julio . . .

5. Anatoli decided to have a **revel** because . . .

6. Megumi decided to **embellish** her mountain bike by . . .

7. After Jim made a **wanton** remark, Sheila . . .

8. When we saw how **gaunt** the dog was, we . . .

9. Because the rumors were **insidious**, Ameer . . .

10. We were shocked to see Adela wearing a **garish** shirt because . . .

Explore It

You know the word *gaunt* by now, but are you familiar with two of its most common synonyms, *lanky* and *lean*? Even though they are synonyms of *gaunt*, each word means something slightly different.

gaunt = skinny and unhealthy looking

lanky = tall and thin

lean = thin but strong

> Working with someone else, read the story below and write the answers down on a separate piece of paper. Remember that each of the three words should be used only once. Be prepared to share your work.

> The track team was preparing for its big meet. Gina, who had the 1. ____ body of a marathon runner, stretched until her muscles felt loose. Paul, the team captain, was dreading the meet. He had been sick all week and looked 2. ____ and unprepared for the race. Unlike Paul, Carlos was excited about the meet. He was the team's pole vaulter. Carlos was so tall and skinny that he flew easily over the high bar. For Carlos, having a 3. ____ body was an advantage!

My, How Things Have CHANGED!

Technology is changing every day. Just think—the Internet didn't even exist 50 years ago. Today, people all around the world communicate with each other online! Read on to find out how technology and people's opinions of technology have changed over the years.

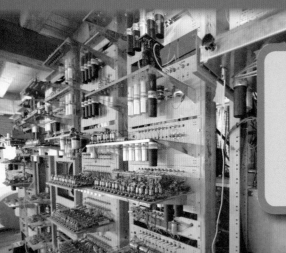

Then
The first computer would not have been described as gaunt. That's because it weighed more than a male elephant!

Now
Today's computers are not as garish as the computers of the past. Many laptops weigh less than 10 pounds!

Then
The first cell phone weighed more than 2 pounds. It also had fewer embellishments than cell phones have today but was sold for nearly $4,000!

Now
Many cell phones today weigh less than 100 grams, which is about the weight of 100 paper clips!

Then

In the 1940s, some people believed that television would not be popular in the future because staring at a box every night would become monotonous.

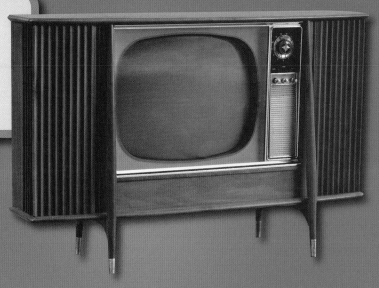

Now

Nearly 99 percent of people in the United States own televisions. If the inventors of the first TV knew just how popular their device had become, they'd be reveling in its success.

Then

In 1903, the president of a bank predicted that automobiles were nothing more than a silly fad and that people would soon return to a better form of transportation—horses.

Now

Let's just say teenagers aren't lining up to get their very first horse and wagon. By the early 21st century, there were about 140 million cars in the United States alone.

Rev Up Your Writing

You've just read about how technology has changed over time. Write about a type of technology that you think will change in the future. Will an existing high-tech tool get even better? Will a new invention change the world forever? Use as many of the vocabulary words as possible but make sense.

Word Organizer

Copy this graphic organizer onto a separate piece of paper.

Think of words that describe things that are monotonous and write your answers in the ovals. Then give examples of things that are monotonous and write your answers in the boxes. Explain your answers.

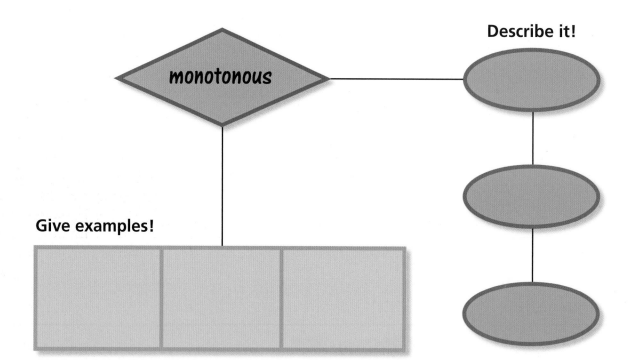

Give Me the
Truth!

Urban legends are a kind of folklore. Many people believe some of these insidious lies. However, some of the outrageous stories you read are actually true! Read the two stories below. Only one story is true. Can you separate fact from fiction?

Ferocious Fur

Another story claims that in 1998, a group of British animal lovers freed some 6,000 minks that were living on a mink farm. The animal lovers had intended to save the poor creatures from becoming the latest furry shroud on the next celebrity. However, driven by their profuse hunger and natural curiosity, the minks raided the town, killing many domestic pets and wild animals. In defense, residents took drastic measures. Many minks were killed—the very outcome the animal lovers had been trying to avoid.

Flesh-Eating Bananas

One story claims that in 2000, several shipments of Costa Rican bananas were infected with a flesh-eating bacteria. A banana's skin is not impermeable, so the bacteria were able to penetrate through the skin and into the fruit. Doctors warned that people infected with the bacteria would come down with a fever and a skin infection. Soon after, the bacteria would begin to eat two to three centimeters of skin per hour!

Hint: The true story has a title that uses a literary device known as *alliteration*.

The Human Lightning Rod

"Lightning never strikes the same place twice."

Many people around the world believe this popular saying to be true. Park ranger Roy Sullivan, however, was not one of these people. That's because Sullivan was struck by lightning, not once, not twice, but seven times!

The "Human Lightning Rod," as Sullivan was sometimes called, developed quite a reputation during his life. Between the years of 1942–1977, lightning seemed to find Sullivan. Some people might think that Sullivan wantonly put himself at risk, but that's not the case. He was just unlucky enough to get struck seven times.

Sullivan's injuries were rarely severe. The first time he was struck by lightning, in 1942, one of his toenails fell off. The fourth lightning strike set his hair on fire.

People say lightning doesn't strike the same place twice. Unfortunately for the Human Lightning Rod, it looks like there's no rule about how often lightning can strike the same person!

Rev Up Your Writing

You've just read some incredible stories—some true and some not. Write about an unbelievable story that you've heard. Is the story true or is it a hoax? Use as many of the vocabulary words as possible but make sense.

Can You Relate?

Copy this graphic organizer onto a separate piece of paper. Match the following words with their related vocabulary word. If a word relates to more than one vocabulary word, explain why.

exquisite   Something that is exquisite is beautiful and delicate.
flamboyant   If someone is flamboyant, he or she is flashy and proud of it.
florid   Something that is florid is very fancy and has too much decoration.
innumerable   If you have an innumerable amount of something, you have too much to count.
prolific   If something is prolific, it produces a lot.

embellishment	garish	profuse

In Your Own Words

Respond to one of the following prompts on a separate piece of paper. As you respond, use as many of the vocabulary words as possible. Be creative but make sense!

▶ Write about a time when you or someone you know went to an unusual party or other event. Describe what happened at the event and what was so strange about it.

▶ Write a poem about someone who went through a difficult experience and survived. What happened to the person? How did he or she survive?

▶ Write about a topic of your choice.

VOCABULARY

profuse
impermeable
shrouded
monotonous
revel
embellishment
wanton
gaunt
insidious
garish

207

Glossary

A

abashed (uh BASHT) If you are abashed, you feel ashamed and embarrassed.

abate (uh BAYT) If something abates, it becomes less intense or widespread.

abide (uh BYD) When you abide by a rule, you accept it and follow it.

affix (uh FIHKS) When something is affixed, it is attached to something else.

altruistic (AL tru IHS tihk) Altruistic people take care of other people's needs before they take care of their own.

ameliorate (uh MEEL yuh rayt) Someone who ameliorates a situation makes it better or easier.

apathy (AP uh thee) Apathy is a lack of interest in or enthusiasm about anything.

apparition (AP uh RIHSH uhn) An apparition is something that looks like a ghost.

arbitrary (AHR buh TREHR ee) An arbitrary action or decision is made without any good reason.

arduous (AHR ju uhs) An arduous task takes a lot of effort.

artifice (AHR tuh fihs) Artifice is the skillful and clever use of tricks, such as disguises, to fool others.

ascend (uh SEHND) Something that ascends moves upward.

assiduously (uh SIHJ u uhs lee) When you do something assiduously, you put a lot of effort and hard work into it.

atone (uh TOHN) When you atone for something that you did wrong, you do something to make up for it.

avert (uh VURT) When you avert something, you keep it from happening.

awry (uh RY) If something goes awry, it fails to happen in the way it was planned.

B

banal (buh NAHL) Someone or something that is banal is so common that it is boring.

bereavement (bih REEV muhnt) Bereavement is the feeling of pain and loss you experience when a close friend or family member dies.

brazenly (BRAY zuhn lee) When you do something brazenly, you do it openly even though you know it's wrong.

brooding (BROO dihng) Brooding is used to describe a threatening and disturbing feeling.

C

capitulate (kuh PIHCH uh layt) When you capitulate, you give up and surrender.

caustic (KAWS tihk) Someone or something that is caustic is so harsh that it damages whatever it comes into contact with.

censor (SEHN suhr) Someone who censors something removes any part of it that is thought to be harmful or dangerous.

chagrin (shuh GRIHN) Chagrin is a feeling of embarrassment because you failed.

compensate (KOM puhn sayt) When you compensate someone, you try to make up for something lost or stolen.

congregate (KONG gruh gayt) When people congregate, they come together in a group.

conjecture (kuhn JEHK chuhr) A conjecture is an opinion you form without much proof.

covet (KUHV iht) If you covet something, you want it for yourself.

cower (KOW uhr) If a person or animal cowers, it crouches and moves back because it is afraid.

credible (KREHD uh buhl) Someone or something that is credible can be trusted or believed.

croon (kroon) When you croon, you sing in a gentle and pleasant way.

curtail (kur TAYL) When you curtail something, such as the amount of money you spend, you reduce it.

D

debunk (dee BUHNGK) If you debunk some idea or belief that people have, you show proof that it is not true or real.

deference (DEHF uhr uhns) When you show deference, you act in a way that shows a deep respect for someone or something.

degrade (dih GRAYD) If you degrade someone or something, you damage its value or reputation.

demure (dih MYUR) A demure person is quiet and shy.

deplete (dih PLEET) When supplies are depleted, they are completely used up.

despotic (dehs POT ihk) A despotic person uses his or her powers over others in an unfair and often cruel way.

deteriorate (dih TIHR ee uh rayt) If something deteriorates, its condition gets worse and worse.

devotion (dih VOH shuhn) Devotion is a deep love and admiration for someone or something.

disconsolate (dihs KON suh liht) A disconsolate person is so sad he or she can't be cheered up.

disparity (dihs PAR uh tee) If there is a disparity between two things, there is a difference between them.

disregard (DIHS rih GAHRD) If you disregard something, you decide it is not worth paying attention to.

E

effusive (ih FYOO sihv) Effusive people show their feelings with a lot of enthusiasm.

egregious (ih GREE juhs) An egregious act is shockingly bad.

elude (ih LOOD) If you elude something that is chasing you, you escape from it using cleverness and skill.

embellishment (ehm BEHL ihsh muhnt) An embellishment is a decoration that is added to something to make it seem more attractive.

embolden (ehm BOHL duhn) If you feel emboldened by something, you suddenly have the confidence to act boldly and bravely.

enamored (ehn AM uhrd) When you are enamored with someone, you are fascinated by or in love with that person.

epitome (ih PIHT uh mee) The epitome of something is the best example or model of it.

err (ehr) If you err, you make a mistake.

expanse (ehk SPANS) An expanse is a wide, open area.

explicit (ehk SPLIHS iht) Something that is explicit is explained so clearly that it can't possibly be misunderstood.

F

fabrication (FAB ruh KAY shuhn) A fabrication is something that is created, not natural.

fastidious (fas TIHD ee uhs) Fastidious people are extremely neat and picky about details.

flagrant (FLAY gruhnt) A flagrant act is something very bad that is done without any attempt to hide it.

flushed (fluhsht) When you are flushed, your face turns red.

formidable (FAWR muh duh buhl) If someone or something is formidable, you feel threatened by its size or strength.

fraudulent (FRAW juh luhnt) If someone's words or actions are fraudulent, they are meant to be false or dishonest.

furtive (FUR tihv) Furtive people are secretive and sneaky because they are trying to hide what they are doing.

G

garish (GAIR ihsh) When something is garish, it is so flashy and colorful that it's ugly.

garrulous (GAR uh luhs) Garrulous people talk a lot, especially about unimportant things.

gaunt (gahnt) A person who is gaunt is very skinny and unhealthy looking.

gingerly (JIHN juhr lee) When you do something gingerly, you do it carefully because you are nervous about making a mistake or getting hurt.

gnarled (nahrld) Something that is gnarled is wrinkled and twisted, usually because it is old.

grueling (GROOL ihng) A grueling experience is so difficult it exhausts you.

H

hierarchy (HY uh RAHR kee) A hierarchy is a way of ranking group members based on their importance.

I

ignoble (ihg NOH buhl) Something that is ignoble is dishonorable and has a bad reputation.

ignominiously (IHG nuh MIHN ee uhs lee) If you behave ignominiously, you do something that is shameful and disgraceful.

illicit (ih LIHS iht) An illicit activity is illegal or not allowed.

immaculate (ih MAK yuh liht) Something that is immaculate is spotlessly clean.

immobile (ih MOH buhl) Something that is immobile can't be moved.

impermeable (ihm PUR mee uh buhl) If something is impermeable, it is impossible to enter it or break through it.

implausible (ihm PLAW zuh buhl) A story that is implausible is so unlikely that it's hard to believe.

implication (IHM pluh KAY shuhn) An implication is the unspoken meaning or message behind what you say or do.

incandescent (IHN kuhn DEHS uhnt) If something is incandescent, it shines brightly.

incipient (ihn SIHP ee uhnt) Something that is incipient is just beginning to happen.

inclination (IHN kluh NAY shuhn) If you have an inclination about something, you have a feeling about it that helps you make a decision.

incomprehensible (IHN kom prih HEHN suh buhl) When someone or something is incomprehensible, it is impossible to understand.

incongruous (ihn KONG gru uhs) If something is incongruous, it seems strange because it is out of place.

inevitable (ihn EHV uh tuh bul) If something is inevitable, it's going to happen no matter what.

ingratiate (ihn GRAY shee ayt) When you ingratiate yourself to others, you do things to try to get them to like you.

inhabit (ihn HAB uht) If you inhabit a place, you live there.

iniquity (ih NIHK wuh tee) An iniquity is a situation or act that is unfair or wicked.

innocuous (ih NOK yu uhs) Something that is innocuous won't hurt you because it is harmless.

insidious (ihn SIHD ee uhs) You use insidious to describe something harmful that spreads slowly without being noticed.

integral (IHN tuh gruhl) Something that is an integral part of something else is absolutely necessary for it to work.

inverted (ihn VUR tihd) Something that is inverted is upside down or opposite from what it usually is.

J

jettison (JEHT uh suhn) When you jettison something, you get rid of it because it is not needed or is causing a problem.

L

loiter (LOY tuhr) When you loiter somewhere, you stay there without any good reason.

lull (luhl) If something lulls you, it makes you feel calm and sleepy.

M

mainstay (MAYN STAY) A mainstay is the most important part of something, the part that supports everything else.

malicious (muh LIHSH uhs) A malicious person wants to hurt others or cause them pain.

meager (MEE guhr) When there is a meager amount of something, there is very little of it.

mellifluous (muh LIHF lu uhs) Something that sounds mellifluous sounds pleasant and smooth.

mock (mok) Someone who mocks you imitates you in order to make fun of you.

molten (MOHL tuhn) If something is molten, it has been melted into a liquid by extreme heat.

monotonous (muh NOT uh nuhs) When something is monotonous, it is very boring because it never changes.

murky (MUR kee) If something is murky, it is dark and difficult to see through.

muse (myooz) When you muse about something, you think about it deeply.

mutate (MYOO tayt) If something mutates, it changes into some new, usually strange, form.

myriad (MIHR ee uhd) If you have myriad things, you have a very large number of them.

N

nostalgic (nos TAL jihk) When you feel nostalgic, you remember a happier time in the past.

O

oblige (uh BLYJ) If you oblige someone, you do something for that person because you want to, not because you have to.

obliterate (uh BLIHT uh rayt) When you obliterate something, you completely destroy it.

odyssey (OD uh see) An odyssey is a long, eventful journey.

P

pan (pan) If you pan an area, you look slowly across it from side to side.

patronizingly (PAY truh nyz ihng lee) People who act patronizingly toward you treat you like they are smarter or better than you are.

petulant (PEHCH uh luhnt) A petulant person is grouchy and often gets angry over things that aren't important.

phenomenon (fuh NOM uh non) A phenomenon is a rare or unusually important event.

pivotal (PIHV uh tuhl) A pivotal event is extremely important and can completely change the way things turn out.

plaintive (PLAYN tihv) A plaintive sound or expression is sad and shows regret.

possess (puh ZEHS) If you possess something, you own it and control it.

postulate (POS chuh layt) When you postulate something, you make an educated guess that it is true.

preoccupied (pree OK yuh pyd) When you're preoccupied with something, you are thinking about it so much that you don't notice other things.

presumptuous (prih ZUHMP chu uhs) If you are presumptuous, you decide that you have the right to do things that are none of your business.

profound (pruh FOWND) A profound feeling or experience affects you deeply.

profuse (pruh FYOOS) If there is a profuse amount of something, there is a lot of it.

prudence (PROO duhns) When you show prudence, you plan things carefully and wisely.

Q

quaint (kwaynt) If something is quaint, it is old-fashioned and charming.

R

rapt (rapt) If you are rapt, something amazes you and captures your attention.

receptive (rih SEHP tihv) Someone who is receptive is open to new ideas and experiences.

redolent (REHD uh luhnt) If something is redolent of something else, it reminds you of that thing.

regale (rih GAYL) If you regale someone, you entertain him or her with stories.

relentless (rih LEHNT lihs) Something that is relentless keeps going on and on for a very long time.

replete (rih PLEET) Something that is replete is almost completely filled.

reproach (rih PROHCH) When you reproach someone, you criticize that person for doing something wrong.

resilient (rih ZIHL ee uhnt) If you are resilient, you recover quickly from something bad that happened to you.

retaliate (rih TAL ee AYT) When you retaliate, you get revenge for something that someone has done to you.

retrospect (REHT ruh spehkt) When you think about something in retrospect, you think back on it and may change your opinion about it.

revel (REHV uhl) A revel is a loud celebration.

S

saucy (SAW see) Someone who is saucy is rude in a playful way.

scour (skowr) When you scour something, you scrub it in order to clean it.

shrouded (shrowd ehd) If someone or something has been shrouded, it has been covered, usually with a cloth.

skeptical (SKEHP tuh kuhl) If you are skeptical about something, you doubt that it's true.

somber (SOM buhr) When you are somber, you feel sad and gloomy.

stricken (STRIHK uhn) If you are stricken with something, you are suffering from it.

strident (STRY duhnt) A strident sound is harsh and unpleasant to listen to.

stymie (STY mee) If you are stymied by something, you just don't know what to do about it.

subjection (suhb JEHK shuhn) When people are forced into subjection, they are brought under complete control.

submissive (suhb MIHS ihv) Submissive people quietly do what others tell them to do.

substantial (suhb STAN shuhl) When there is a substantial amount of something, there is a lot of it.

succumb (suh KUHM) If you succumb to something, you can't fight it anymore so you just give up.

sullen (SUHL uhn) A person who is sullen is bad-tempered and unfriendly.

supple (SUHP uhl) Something that is supple is soft and bends easily.

T

tacit (TAS iht) Something that is tacit is understood or agreed upon without having to talk about it.

taciturn (TAS uh turn) Taciturn people may seem unfriendly because they don't talk very much.

taunt (tawnt) A person who taunts you annoys or teases you in order to be hurtful.

tenacious (tih NAY shuhs) A tenacious person is very tough and doesn't give up easily.

torrent (TAWR uhnt) A torrent is a large amount of fast and furiously flowing water.

transitory (TRAN suh TAWR ee) If something is transitory, it only lasts for a moment.

U

unattainable (UHN uh TAY nuh buhl) Something that is unattainable is impossible to get.

unprecedented (uhn PREHS uh DEHN tihd) If something is unprecedented, it has never happened before.

unwieldy (uhn WEEL dee) Something that is unwieldy is hard to handle because of its awkward weight or size.

utter (UHT uhr) When you utter a word or sound, you say it.

V

virtuous (VUR chu uhs) Someone who is virtuous has high morals and always does the right thing.

volition (voh LIHSH uhn) When you act on your own volition, you have the power and freedom to make your own decisions.

W

wan (won) People who look wan look pale because they are weak or worn out.

wanton (WON tuhn) A wanton action causes harm to someone or something on purpose without any reason.

writhe (ryth) When you writhe, you twist and turn because of extreme pain or shame.

Acknowledgments

Grateful acknowledgment is given to the following sources for illustrations and photography:

Illustration

P.15 Stan Gorman; p.18 Capucine Mazille; pp.21-22, 25 Diana Kizlauskas; pp.34-35, 38 Tom McNeely; pp.47, 50 Lin Wang; pp.59-60, 63 Joel Spector; p.69 Angela Ehrhard; pp.72-73 Dom Lee; p.79 Judith Hunt; p.82 Sholto Walker; pp.84-85, 89 Bob Doucet; p.92 Maria Eugenia; p.104 Beth Griffis Johnson; pp.110, 113 Aaron Jasinski; pp.116-117 Richard Stergulz; p.119 Steve Haefele; p.129 Doug Holgate; pp.135-136, 138 Robert Sauber; pp.170-171, 174 Lyle Miller; p.181 Jeff Crosby; pp.183, 187 Winson Trang; p.191 Helle Urban; pp.193-194 Melissa Grimes; pp.196-197, 199 Hrana Janto.

Photography

P.8 ©Andrew Eccles/JBG Photo; p.9 ©Martyn Colbeck/photolibrary; p.12 ©Caroline Mackenzie/Woodfin Camp/Getty Images; p.16b ©Photodisc/Getty Images; p.16c ©Robert Glusic/Corbis; p.16d ©Digital Vision/Getty Images; p.18 ©maxstockphoto/shutterstock; p.28a ©Vera Devai/epa/Corbis; p.28b ©Alistaircotton/Dreamstime.com; p.31b ©Stephen Frink/Photographer's Choice/Getty Images; p.32c ©Kevin Schafer/zefa/Corbis; p.32d ©John Arnold/shutterstock; p.41a ©Daniela Illing/shutterstock; p.41d ©The Detroit News; p.41e ©The Heidelberg Project; p.42a ©Daniela Illing/shutterstock; p.42b-e Sam Dudgeon/HRW; p.44a ©Jin Yin Hua; p.44b Coneyl Jay/Science Photo Library; p.45a-c ©Willard Wigan; p.48 ©Comstock; p.54c ©Corbis Royalty Free Photography/Fotosearch; p.56a ©Gerald Kooyman/Corbis; p.57 ©Michael Lok/iStockphoto; p.67 ©Photos 12/Alamy; p.70a ©imagebroker/Alamy; p.70b ©Judith Collins/Alamy; p.70c ©Sabine Duerichen/LOOK/GettyImages; p.75 ©Jonathan Slaff/Ovoworks, Inc; p.78a ©Dar Yang Yan/iStockphoto; p.79a ©The Granger Collection, NY.jpg; p.79b ©Werner Forman/Art Resource, NY; p.81b ©David R. Frazier Photolibrary, Inc./Alamy; p.95a Courtesy of Ryan's Well Foundation www.ryanswell.ca; p.95b ©Ryan's Well Foundation; p.95c ©Jon Muresan for www.volvoforlifeawards.com; p.96a ©Nicola Karle; p.98 ©VEER Antonio Barbagallo/Getty Images; p.99 ©Hulton Archive/Getty Images; p.101 ©1999-2006 Richard Corben/Steve Niles/Rob Zombie/IDW Publishing; p.104a ©2005 Getty Images; p.104b ©Image Source Pink/2005 Getty Images; p.104c ©David Toase/Getty Images; p.105b ©Travel Ink/Getty Images; p.105c ©George Steinmetz/Corbis; p.107a ©istockphoto; p.107b ©Ahmad Faizal Yahya/istockphoto; p.107c ©Ryan McVay/Getty Images; p.108a ©iStockphoto; p.108b ©2007 Oakley Cochran/Alaskastock.com; p.108c ©Tim MacPherson/Stone/GettyImages; p.111 ©Getty Images; p.120a ©Comstock Images/PictureQuest; p.120b ©Christian Darkin/Photo Researchers, Inc; p.122 ©AFP/Getty Images; p.123 ©Design Pics Inc./Alamy; p.126 ©Jon Hrusa/epa/CORBIS; p.130d ©SuperStock/Alamy; p.132 ©Andrew Gunners/Getty Images; p.133a ©Photodisc Collection/Getty Images; p.133b ©Tom Brakefield/Getty Images; p.133c ©Digital Vision/Getty Images; p.133d ©Tom Brakefield/Getty Images; p.133e ©Andrew Gunners/Getty Images; p.141 ©Associated Press/Bill Wolf; p.142a ©Dynamic Graphics Group/Creatas/Alamy; p.144 ©Photodisc Royalty Free Photograph/Fotosearch; p.147 ©Popperfoto/Alamy; pp.148, 150 ©Comstock; p.153a ©Mike Kemp/Getty Images; p.153b ©Photodisc Royalty Free Photography/Fotosearch; p.153c ©Catherine dée Auvi/iStockphoto; p.153d ©The International Spy Museum; p.154a ©Mike Kemp/Getty Images; p.154b ©Joe Brandt/iStockphoto; p.154c ©Willi Schmitz/iStockphoto; p.156a ©Jacom Stephens/iStockphoto; p.156b ©Robert Kyllo/shutterstock; p.156d ©Digital Vision/Getty Images; p.159a ©Nic Taylor/iStockphoto; p.159b ©G.E. Kidder Smith/Corbis; p.159c ©Frost Lee/Imagestate/Photolibrary; p.160 ©Nancy Carter/NorthWind Picture Archives/NorthWind; p.161 ©Jeff Greenberf/Alamy; p.164 ©Chris Nash/Getty Images; p.165 ©Noshir Desai/Corbis; p.167a ©Chen Ping Hung/shutterstock; p.167b ©Michael Rougier/Getty Images; p.167c ©Paul Broadbent/Alamy; p.168a ©Chen Ping Hung/shutterstock; p.168b ©fStop/Alamy; p.177a ©Geoffrey Black/istockphoto; p.177b ©Gregory Shaver/Associated Press; p.178a, b ©ajt/shutterstock; p.178c ©mihaicalin/shutterstock; p.178d ©Bernard Thomas/Associated Press; p.180a ©Cristina Cazan/shutterstock; p.180b ©iStockphoto; p.180d ©Shaun Walker/Associated Press; p.181a ©Jan Rihak/iStockphoto; p.181b ©iStockphoto; p.180c ©1996 Photodisc, Inc; p.184a ©Photodisc/Getty Images; p.184b ©Royalty-Free/CORBIS; p.190a ©Manuel Silvestri/AFP/Getty Images; p.190b ©Associated Press; p.190c ©Luigi Costantini/Associated Press; p.191a ©1993 Photodisc, Inc; pp.193, 194 ©Sean Gladwell/shutterstock; p.202b ©Lawrence Manning/Corbis; p.202c ©Pawel Libera/Corbis; p.203b ©Dynamic Graphics Value/SuperStock; p.205a ©Judith Collins/Alamy; p.205b ©Visual&Written SL/Alamy.

Additional photography by Getty Images Royalty Free; Photodisc/Getty Images; Brand X Pictures/Getty Images; Corbis Royalty Free; Tom Fuller; Patrick Gnan; Masterfile Royalty Free; Comstock Royalty Free.